In Don's Montana
Kitchen

Gluten-Free and Dairy-Free
Gourmet Cooking
From the Edge of the Wilderness

DON DOIG

ISBN: 978-1-4834-8489-1 (sc)
ISBN: 978-1-4834-8488-4 (e)

Lulu Publishing Services rev. date: 04/30/2018

Contents

Acknowledgements

Thanks to Ilo, David, Lynda, Mike, Melinda, Nancy, Tina, Steve, Julia for assistance in editing or testing, for advice and support.

Introduction

If food and cooking have long been important in your life, it can be a daunting task to cook tasty, interesting food when you can no longer eat many of the mainstays of modern or classic cooking. It was for me. Ordinary, pedestrian food has long been of little interest to me, so the trick has been to come up with gluten-free, dairy free food which is also interesting and delicious.

This is a unique cookbook, reflecting more than 40 years in the kitchen, including stints as head chef in several Montana restaurants. It also reflects my personal experiences as a hunter-gatherer, fisherman and gardener. After decades of eating rich French food with lots of butter, cream and cheese, and eating processed non-organic foods loaded with herbicides, I developed gluten sensitivity and also sensitivity to milk protein. Gluten-containing grains include wheat, rye, barley, spelt, kamut, and triticale.

Modern wheat, in particular, has been bred to contain a number of molecules besides the glutens that have negative health consequences. These include wheat germ agglutinin, amylopectin A, and wheat gliadin. It also likely contains toxic glyphosate herbicide. Most people would do well to avoid it.

The book *Dangerous Grains* by Braly and Hoggan estimates gluten-containing grains cause negative health impacts for some 90 million Americans, and constitute a basic cause of illness in about 10 million Americans. These include autoimmune diseases, cancer and osteoporosis. Celiac disease (the best known pathology associated with gluten sensitivity) itself affects about 2 million people.

There are now decent substitutes for wheat in the market for baking, generally mixes of several gluten-free seeds and grains. Organic is highly recommended. Books are available dealing with gluten free baking.

Whenever a recipe here calls for flour, just use your standard gluten free mix. Lately, I have been using Costco's Gluten Free Organic Perfect Flour Blend.

Many gluten-sensitive people also develop intolerance to milk protein, as in my case.

This resulted in major shifts in my diet, besides the obvious changes, it made it nearly impossible to eat most processed foods because of gluten-containing additives and contamination due to things like incomplete distillation of vinegar and grain spirits and contamination of processing equipment. As a result, this has required me to make most things from scratch. I was forced to adopt changes which would benefit anyone.

I have always been healthy, but was overweight. On this diet, I lost more than 70 pounds without really trying. I have made an effort to switch to organic food, out of concern for the toxic, carcinogenic, and otherwise unhealthy foods sold to us by industrial monoculture agriculture and the rest of the corporate food chain. Living in a small isolated Montana community makes it difficult to visit health food stores on anything other than an occasional foray into a larger town. Fortunately, wild game and fish are available for those willing to go get them. Where the recipes call for game or trout, you can adapt these recipes for organic grass-fed beef and lamb, organic free range chickens and pork, or wild-caught ocean fish (if not contaminated by radiation or toxic waste) or other wild caught fish. In addition to growing a big organic garden, I forage for wild mushrooms and other edible plants.

Much of this cookbook revolves around sauces, whether incorporated into the dish as it cooks, or as a stand-alone sauce added to meats once they are cooked.

While this is not a paleo cookbook, many of the recipes will be of interest to those on a paleo diet.

I partly shifted to oriental cuisines, in which I had long had an interest, and experience with cooking. Chinese, Indian and Thai cuisines, primarily. I like food which has lots of flavor – complex flavors, often hot and spicy. Heat is, of course, adjustable... :) Some of these recipes are essentially fusions between western (French- inspired) cuisine and oriental influences.

The major breakthrough in my adaptation occurred when I discovered that coconut oil could substitute for butter in most applications. I use organic virgin coconut oil which is solid at 76 degrees and good for frying to 350 degrees. It doesn't taste like butter, but it is delicious in its own right.

Happily, coconut oil turns out to be a health food superfood with all kinds of benefits to your health. For one thing, it lowers the bad cholesterol and raises the good cholesterol and promotes brain health.

Similarly, coconut milk (thick or thin) can nicely substitute for cream and milk. Cultured coconut milk is an acceptable substitute for yoghurt. The one big thing is I have found no decent commercial cheese substitutes. What there is, is made with unfermented soy, and that is said to be unhealthy and they often contain casein (milk) protein, and besides there are none that even claim to substitute for Swiss, Gruyere, or blue cheese. However, raw cashew butter can be used in coconut cream sauces or pizza toppings for a cheesy effect . With these changes, acceptable and quite delicious quasi-French food becomes possible once again. Coconut manna is very finely pureed coconut meat, it can be purchased, or it can be made, with some diligence, with a powerful blender.

When using the recipes in this cookbook, note that reference is made to other recipes in this book. It was too expensive to cross-reference with numbers, so check out the Index where indicated with an *.

Basic Kitchen Procedures

Abbreviations

tsp = teaspoon; Tb = tablespoon; lb = pound

Preserving

I preserve fresh herbs from the garden by briefly parboiling them (30-60 seconds), refresh in cold water, drain and lightly press. Freeze in 1 tsp – 1+ Tb packets. I use wax paper for the first layer and wrap that in aluminum foil. Put the foil packets in a baggie and label and date it. This preserves the fresh flavor but stops the autolytic enzymes from turning it to mush over time in the freezer.

I preserve peppers by slicing them and sautéing briefly in coconut oil, and freezing in packets suitable for a single dish (I do packets generally around 1/2 cup) in which they can be used as fresh peppers. I have also preserved leeks in this manner.

I store part of the tomato harvest in the form of slow-roasted tomato slices, coarsely chopped in the food processor, and frozen in small jars. I store garlic as roasted garlic paste in olive oil or coconut oil, frozen in small jars.

If you don't yet have a garden, a good strategy is to buy quantities of fresh produce in season at your local farmer's markets and freeze them as above.

Best practices should always be followed, including the use of fresh-ground spices, fresh herbs, filtered water, etc. Better quality ingredients yield superior results. Organic, non-GMO food tastes better and avoids the toxicity, carcinogenicity, etc. of herbicides and pesticides, and the proven harmful effects of GMO food such as cancer. Incidentally, when examining the health effects of such things as herbicides, pesticides, and GMOs, consider the source of the funding of published research. He who pays the piper calls the tune.

While it is important that all foods be cooked optimally, some foods are especially sensitive to overcooking. Not only is texture affected (either too mushy or too tough or dry), but with liver, duck breast, asparagus, spinach, peas and broccoli, the flavor itself changes for the worse if they are greatly overcooked.

Asparagus, for instance, responds well to being peeled to remove the fibers in the outer portion of the stalk, so it can be cooked quickly, in a matter of a few minutes. Also you get to use more of the stalk.

Broccoli stems can also be peeled.

Soy sauce usually has wheat added to it. If you can't find a good gluten-free soy sauce, use gluten-free Tamari sauce, or coconut aminos. Distilled vinegar may be a problem for sensitive people.

Alcoholic spirits distilled from gluten-containing grains (grain spirits) may contain enough gluten contaminants from incomplete distillation that it can be a problem for sensitive people. Beware of inexpensive brandies, etc. that may be cut with grain spirits. In addition, many American brandies are aged in old whiskey barrels.

Several recipes in this book call for Huckleberry jam or syrup. This specifically refers to wild mountain huckleberries found in the northern Rockies. This is available online or in some stores. The closest commercial alternative is boysenberry.

How to Boil Water: Even the water you use makes a difference. I use filtered water (using a Berkey Light water filter) which makes tap water taste much better and eliminates toxins like fluoride, chlorine, glyphosate (Roundup), and the myriad of other contaminants tap water commonly has. By the way, have you ever tasted hot tap water from the hot water heater? *Aack!* If you need hot water to cook with or consume, boil filtered water.

When "onions" are called for, I mean yellow cooking onions unless otherwise specified.

If you are a gardener, garlic scapes are the young flower stalks that need to be removed to promote bulb development. Harvest them as soon as you notice them, well before the flowers open. They have a mild garlic flavor and can be cut up and added to stir-fries, etc.

Things to have on hand

I keep on hand homemade gluten-free and dairy-free condiments prepared in advance that can be used to make quick and easy secondary sauces, such as the Hot Chocolate Chili Garlic Sauce for venison made with Hot Sweet Chili Garlic Sauce* plus chocolate. Mustards, chutneys, ketchups, etc. can be used creatively in this manner. Helen Witty's *The Good Stuff Cookbook* is a good source for recipes for mustards, condiments, relishes, sauces etc. which you can adapt to gluten-free and dairy-free. I try to keep on hand jars of frozen stocks and bone broths*.

Xylitol is an alternative plant-derived 5 carbon sugar that is metabolized along different pathways than those used by glucose and fructose (and sucrose), pathways independent of insulin regulation. It also has fewer calories. It is substituted 1:1 for sucrose, or table sugar.

I also sometimes combine it with stevia. If a recipe would normally call for brown sugar, I add a little organic molasses.

I generally use avocado oil when high-temperature frying is called for. It is generally thought to be healthy, unlike things like canola oil.

Roasted Cumin Seeds

Roast whole cumin seeds on the stovetop in a small dry cast iron skillet until they begin to smoke and darken.

Let cool then grind in a coffee grinder (devoted to spices) or with a mortar and pestle. Best used immediately.

Roasted Szechuan Peppercorns

Roast whole Szechuan peppercorns on the stovetop in a small dry cast iron skillet until they begin to smoke.

Shake occasionally or stir. While they are heating, I use tweezers to remove any stems (they will usually be loose). Grind with a mortar and pestle.

Roasted Garlic Puree

Crush and peel, place in a baking pan coated heavily with coconut oil.

Cover with oiled parchment paper.

Bake about 1 hour at 325 degrees.

Puree in a food processor with olive or coconut oil.

Freeze in 1/2 cup or one cup canning jars.

Roasted Tomatoes

Slice 1/2" to 1" thick. Place in a baking pan coated with coconut oil. Salt lightly. Bake 1 ½ to 2 hours at 325 degrees until well reduced and somewhat caramelized. Chop finely and bottle in 1 cup canning jars. Freeze.

Appetisers

Avocado Dip

Combine

>2 ripe avocados, peeled and diced
>1/2 cup vegan or coconut mayonnaise
>1/4 cup diced scallions or chives
>1/4 cup roasted almond meal
>1 Tb lemon juice
>1 tsp lemon zest
>1 Tb lime juice
>1 tsp lime zest
>1/4 cup chopped roasted tomato*
>1/2 tsp roasted garlic puree*
>1/2 tsp ancho chili powder
>1/2 tsp black pepper
>1/2 tsp garam masala spice mixture
>1 tsp salt

Refrigerate for 2 or more hours. Serve with gluten free crackers or chips, or sliced carrots or celery.

Avocado Pineapple Dip

>2 ripe avocados, peeled
>1 cup pineapple, chopped
>2 Tb salsa
>1/4 cup coconut mayonnaise*
>1 tsp ancho chili powder
>1/2 tsp freshly ground black pepper
>1/2 tsp salt

Place the avocados, pineapple, salsa, mayonnaise, pepper, and salt in the food processor with the metal blade. Process until it is blended but still slightly chunky.

The spoon knife I describe on page 37 comes in handy to separate the avocado flesh from the skin.

Serve with chips or vegetable crudités.

Bacon-Wrapped Pickled Watermelon Rind

1 cup pickled watermelon rind (*The Joy of Cooking* has a recipe, or you can buy it)
1 lb bacon
1 Tb Hot Sweet Chili Garlic Sauce*
Round toothpicks
Aluminum foil, Wax paper or parchment, lightly oiled

Place a sheet of aluminum foil in a broiling pan, and a piece of lightly oiled wax paper on top of that. Preheat the oven on Broil. Cut the bacon in thirds, wrap ½ x 1" pieces of pickled watermelon rind, and secure/ skewer with a toothpick. Place on the wax paper.

Broil for about 12 minutes until brown (keep an eye on it). Top with the Hot Sweet Chili Garlic Sauce (optional) and cook for a couple of minutes more, or pass the sauce separately in a small bowl.

Black Bean Dip

1 can organic black beans, drained
1 tsp roasted garlic puree*
1/4 cup roasted tomato puree*
2 Tb Kalamata olives

1 Tb fresh basil, chopped
2 scallions, sliced
2-4 hot peppers such as serranos or jalapenos, deseeded and sliced
1 tsp white wine vinegar
1/2 tsp ground roasted cumin
1/2 tsp salt
1/2 tsp freshly ground black pepper

Combine all the ingredients and grind in the food processor, leaving some texture.

Refrigerate for at least two hours before serving.

Serve with chips or carrot slabs, celery sticks, etc.

Chicken Liver Spread

1 onion, cut into 1/2 inch dice.

Saute onion in

1/3 cup coconut oil until brown.

Remove onions and add

2 lb chicken livers, diced 1/2"

Cook until brown and combine with onions and

1 Tb raspberry vinegar
2 Tb Madeira wine
1 tsp salt
1/2 tsp black pepper
1 tsp ancho chili powder
2 tsp roasted garlic

1/2 cup vegan or homemade coconut mayonnaise*

2/3 cup chicken stock heated and combined with 1 ½ Tb gelatin. (Sprinkle gelatin on 3 Tb cold stock to moisten, then add the rest of the stock, heated to a boil. Stir thoroughly to dissolve.)

Puree in a food processor until smooth. Taste for salt to taste. Refrigerate to set up, at least 2 hours.

Don's Salsa with Tomatoes and Fruit

Combine

1 quart tomatoes, diced

1 ripe peach or mango or 1+ c. Pineapple, diced

1 medium red onion, diced

2 tsp roasted garlic puree*

1/2 c. chopped basil

1+ minced fresh hot pepper

1 tsp ground chipotle pepper

1 tsp ground cayenne

1/2 tsp Dave's Insanity Sauce, or more cayenne

1 tsp ground ancho chili pepper

1/2 tsp fresh ground black pepper

2 tsp fresh ground toasted cumin seeds

2 tsp fresh ground coriander

2 Tb catsup

1 Tb raspberry vinegar

1 Tb raw honey, or use xylitol and/or stevia

1+ tsp salt

Refrigerate 2 hours.

Fusion Salsa

1 Tb chopped ginger
2 cloves chopped garlic (or use 1 tsp roasted garlic puree)
1/2 cup chopped serrano peppers or other hot fresh peppers

Saute in 1 Tb coconut oil until things begin to brown. Add to:

1 quart fresh tomatoes, chopped
1 pint husk cherries, pineapple and/or mango, chopped
1 red onion, chopped
1 tsp tumeric
1/2 cup fresh Thai basil, chopped (or other basil)
1/4 cup cilantro, chopped
2 tsp garam masala spice mixture
Juice and zest from 1/2 lime
3 drops lemongrass essential oil
1 tsp roasted cumin, freshly ground*
1 Tb freshly ground coriander
1/2 tsp freshly ground cardamon seeds
1 Tb honey
1/2 tsp freshly ground black pepper, 1 tsp salt
1+ tsp cayenne or 1/2 tsp Dave's Insanity Sauce
Refrigerate for at least 2 hours.

Garbanzo Bean Chip Dip

1 can organic garbanzo beans
1/2 cup salsa*
1 tsp roasted garlic*
1/2 cup minced Italian parsley
1/2 tsp salt
1 tsp freshly ground black pepper

Drain, then puree the garbanzo beans. Add the remaining ingredients and mix to combine.

Refrigerate for at least two hours. Serve with chips or vegetable crudités.

Grilled Eggplant Dip

2 long oriental eggplants, grilled
2 onions, sliced and grilled
2 red bell peppers, blackened on the grill, peeled
1 tsp roasted garlic puree
1/2 cup roasted tomato
1/4 cup chopped Kalamata olives
1/2 tsp turmeric
1 tsp roasted, ground cumin seeds
1 tsp salt
1 tsp freshly ground black pepper
1 Tb cider vinegar

Combine all the ingredients in a food processor and blend. There should be some texture remaining. Good with chips or vegetable crudités.

Smoked Trout or Salmon Spread

1 cup smoked trout,whitefish, or salmon broken into small pieces (Prep it in good light and make sure there are no remaining bones. :)

3/4 cup vegan or, preferably, homemade coconut mayonnaise*
2 Tb cultured coconut milk
1 Tb lemon juice
2 Tb minced dill or bread-and-butter cucumber pickles

1 tsp roasted garlic puree*
2 tsp Dijon style mustard
1 tsp freshly ground white pepper
Taste for salt

Mix together and refrigerate at least 2 hours.

Venison Heart Pate

1 large or two small venison hearts, cut in 1/2 - 3/4" pieces
1 lb bacon, 1/2" slices
1/4 cup coconut oil
1 cup onion, chopped
1/4 tsp ground bay leaf
1/2 tsp thyme
2 large eggs
2 tsp roasted garlic puree*
1 tsp ancho chili powder
1/4 tsp allspice powder
2 Tb Madeira wine
2 tsp salt
1 tsp freshly ground black pepper
Additional bacon slices to line the mold with.

Grind finely in a food processor. Coat a pate mold or baking dish with coconut oil and lay slices of bacon on the bottom and sides, then place the pate mixture in it. Lay bacon slices on top.

Place the mold in a pan of boiling water, to 1- 1 ½ inches up the side of the mold.

Bake for 1 ½- 2 hours at 350 degrees. The juices should run clear and the loaf should separate from the sides, 175 degrees on a meat thermometer. Pour out the water and let the pate cool. While it cools, place a heavy weight on top. Let it sit for 2-3 days in the refrigerator. It is then ready to unmold and slice for serving.

Smoked Salmon and Chervil Spread

Combine

  1/2 cup fresh chervil herb, chopped
  1/2 cup coconut mayonnaise*
  1/2 cup smoked salmon, broken in small pieces
  4 scallions, chopped
  1 tsp freshly ground black pepper

Serve with crackers or vegetable crudités.

Venison Liver Spread

  1 lb liver cut in 1/2"cubes.
  1 onion cut in 1/2" dice.
  3 cloves minced garlic (or add 2 tsp roasted garlic puree at the end of cooking.

Sauté onion and garlic until brown in

  1/4 cup coconut oil

Remove onions and garlic and add liver to the remaining oil and sauté until the liver is just pink on the inside.

Puree the liver and onion and mix with

  1 Tb raspberry vinegar
  2 Tb cognac or brandy

1 tsp salt

1/2 tsp black pepper

1/4 tsp ground allspice

1/4 tsp freshly grated nutmeg

1/3 cup vegan or homemade coconut mayonnaise*

1/2 cup broken pistachios, to make a layer in the middle.

Optional: 1/2 to 1 tsp truffle oil

Transfer to a coconut-oiled mold, layer with broken pistachios. Refrigerate for at least 2 hours. Unmold (put in a basin of hot water briefly to melt the coconut oil) and serve with gluten-free crackers or toast. You could use beef, pork, or lamb liver instead of venison.

Soups and Stocks

Poultry Stock and Bone Broth

Using 3 pounds of bones and gizzards and hearts from a chicken, or the legs, wings, back, breast bones, gizzards and hearts from game birds. Cut up the bones with poultry shears. For about 1 ½ gallons. If you brown the bones in the oven prior to simmering, you get brown poultry stock. Cover with 2 gallons of filtered water and add

2 onions, coarsly chopped
1 leek, carefully cleaned and sliced
4 cloves garlic, crushed
3 carrots, sliced
1 stalk celery, sliced
1/2 cup dry white wine
1 tsp salt
1/2 cup Italian parsley
Sprig of thyme or 1/2 tsp dried
1 bay leaf
8 peppercorns

Bring to a boil and simmer partly covered for 1 ½ to 2 hours. Strain and degrease. If you cool it overnight, the fat is easy to remove from the top. The stock can be reduced to concentrate it. The bones can be stripped of meat and the meat can be used for some other dish or as a snack.

Bone Broth

If you add 1 Tb white wine vinegar or cider vinegar and simmer covered for at least 24 hours, you get bone broth, which is highly gelatinized and very good for you. The vinegar is not enough to taste, but it helps with extraction of the gelatin. Use a crock pot for this, completely covered.

Basic Venison or Beef Brown Stock

For a 4-5 gallon stock pot.

Cut leg bones into 2-3" sections. A good way to do this (it's a two person job) is with a Sawsall type reciprocating electric saw. Additionally, you can split the sections with a cleaver and leather mallet. I hold the sections with tongs to do this. Put them into a roasting pan and roast at 350 degrees until the sections are nicely brown on all sides (turn once or twice). If you include some browned butchering scraps you will have a richer stock. Browning the bones and meat is what makes this a Brown stock. You want enough meat and bones to pretty well fill the stock pot. The bones from one or two deer will suffice. (If beef bones are all that you have available, they can be used instead.)

Place the browned bones and meat in the stock pot.

Slice three yellow onions and brown them in 1/2 cup avocado oil. Add them to the pot. A leek or two would be good also.

Add

　　2 ribs celery, diced
　　2 large carrots, thick slices
　　1/2 cup roasted tomatoes or use 1 tomato
　　1 onion, chopped
　　4 crushed cloves garlic or 1 Tb roasted garlic puree
　　1 smoked ham hock, parboiled for 5 minutes

Wrapped in cheesecloth and tied with cotton string:

1/2 cup chopped fresh Italian parsley or 2 Tb parboiled frozen
   parsley
2 bay leaves
1 tsp fresh thyme leaves or 1/2 tsp dried
1 tsp black peppercorns
2 allspice berries

Cover with cold filtered water and bring to a boil. Simmer for 3-4 hours partially covered, skimming scum and oil from the surface as it cooks. Stir occasionally to make sure nothing is sticking to the bottom. Strain. If you have used stew meat, you can use that for some other purpose, and the marrow can be eaten.

As with the chicken stock, if you add 1 Tb white wine vinegar and increase the cooking time to 24-48 hours, you then have **bone broth**, which has had the gelatin extracted from the bones and is very nutritious. Simmer covered on very low heat, then strain. A crockpot works well for this.

Fish or Shellfish Stock

1-2 lb fish bones and heads and/or shrimp or crab shells
1 onion, sliced
2-3 carrots, sliced
2 garlic cloves
1 stalk celery, sliced
1/2 cup parsley stems, chopped
2 bay leaves
1/2 cup dry white wine
1 tsp salt
1/2 tsp black peppercorns

Combine all the ingredients in a stock pot. Cover with filtered water and bring to a simmer. Cook for 1- 1 ½ hours, partially covered.

Strain.

The shrimp and crab shells can be browned in avocado oil before being added to the stock. This helps extract maximum flavor.

Vegetable Stock

For a 3 gallon pot

> 2 onions, coarsely chopped
> 2 leeks, carefully cleaned and sliced
> 2 lb carrots, thickly sliced
> 3 ribs celery, chopped
> 1 turnip, coarsely chopped
> 1 parsnip, coarsely chopped
> 4 cloves garlic, crushed but not peeled
> 1 cup coarsely chopped Italian parsley
> 2 bay leaves
> 1 sprig fresh thyme or 1/2 tsp dried
> 1/2 tsp whole black peppercorns
> 3 slices fresh ginger
> 1 tsp salt
> 1 whole allspice berry

Cover with filtered water and bring to a boil. Partially cover and simmer for 1 1/2 hours, then strain.

Freeze in quart or pint jars and maybe a few 8 oz jars.

Cold Zucchini Soup

Combine

>4 cups young zucchini, chopped
>3 cups chicken stock

Cook until the zucchini is tender. Let cool enough to puree.

Add

>1 Tb lemon juice
>1 Tb tamari or soy sauce
>Salt and pepper to taste

Cool.

Just before serving, whisk in

>1 cup thin coconut milk

Check seasonings.

Minutina Soup

Minutina is a cold-tolerant salad green. Once it gets older and a bit fibrous and it's time to harvest it entirely, this is a tasty soup. Substitute spinach or experiment with other greens.

Saute 1 cup chopped onion in

>1 Tb coconut oil
>Cook until lightly brown, then add
>2 cups coarsly chopped minutina

4 cups good chicken broth, or chicken bone broth
1 Tb wild mushroom powder
Bring to a boil and then simmer for 20 minutes. Let cool a bit, then blend. Strain.
Add 1/2 cup of light coconut milk and bring to the simmer.
Salt & pepper to taste
Optional, 1/2+ cup cooked rice (or cooked gluten-free pasta)
Serves two.

Mushroom Soup

1 cup yellow onions, chopped
2 cloves garlic, chopped
1 Tb coconut oil
2 Tb avocado or grapeseed oil

Saute until onions are light brown. Remove and puree in your food processor.

Saute until lightly brown, adding more oil as needed:

2 cups sliced fresh mushrooms, preferably wild, such as chanterelles, sweet tooths, shrimp russula, or morels.
1/2 cup dried cepes, soaked

Return the onions to the pan with the mushrooms and add

4 cups chicken bone broth or good stock
1 cup thin coconut milk (in a box)
1/4 cup chopped fresh Italian parsley
2 Tb chopped fresh tarragon

Simmer 1/2 hour. Add salt & pepper to taste and 1/4 cup canned coconut milk and bring back to the simmer. Serves four.

Duck Soup

After you have made a concentrated duck stock out of a mallard or other wild duck carcass (the duck minus the boneless breasts), debone it and tear the meat into small pieces, save the vegetables and discard the herb bag.

To the meat, add the reserved stock vegetables, chopped, and

- 4 cups concentrated duck
- 3 cups water
- 1 cup thin coconut milk (boxed)
- 2 Tb wild mushroom powder (I've seen this for sale; I make my own using dried stems or older mushrooms, ground in the blender.)
- 1/2 tsp black pepper
- 1/2 cup instant mashed potatoes as a thickener (per James Beard) or use a couple of Tb of coconut roux (page).

Bring to a boil and simmer for 10 minutes.

Taste for salt.

Serve with gluten-free bread sauteed in coconut oil to brown.

Don's Venison Stew

3 lb venison shank meat and neck meat, cut in 1-1½" pieces. (Stew meat is best when it has lots of gristle --tendons and filaments-- and needs to cook 3-4 hours.) Coat with gluten-free flour & salt & pepper.

Brown in 1/3 c. avocado oil. Remove and set aside.

1/2 cup dried (soaked) chopped cêpe mushrooms (King boletes). Squeeze dry and save the water.

1 cup dried (soaked) chopped additional wild mushrooms such as morels or chanterelles or oyster mushrooms or fairy ring mushrooms (Marasmius oreades). Use 1/2 pound fresh wild mushrooms if you have them, including meadow mushrooms (the wild version of supermarket mushrooms) - they grow in my yard.

Dried gourmet wild type mushrooms are available in many supermarkets and other food stores, and sometimes fresh also. It is cheaper to find your own.. :)

Add soaked and/or fresh mushrooms to

> 1 large yellow onion in 1/2" sections
> 6 cloves of garlic, crushed, whole
> 1 leek, 1/2" pieces

Lightly brown in the same pan, adding more oil if needed.

Add

> 2 cups of red wine, and reduce. Then add
> 1 carrot cut in thirds
> 1 stalk celery cut in thirds
> Reserved mushroom soaking liquid
> 1 tsp salt
> 1 herb bouquet (a handful of Italian parsley, fresh or dried thyme, 2 bay leaves, 1/2 tsp whole black peppercorns tied in cheesecloth)
> 8 cups good venison or beef stock
> 1/4 cup brandy or cognac
> One smoked ham hock, split
> Water to cover

Bring to a simmer and let cook for 3 hours, stirring occasionally.

Then remove the carrot and celery pieces and add

3-4 boiling potatoes in 3/4" pieces (or so)
3 carrots in 1/2" slices
2 stalks celery, 1/2" slices
2 turnips, 1/2" pieces
2 parsnips, 1/2" pieces
2 12 oz cans great northern white beans, drained
1, 4 oz can tomato sauce or 2 Tb tomato paste or 1/2 cup tomato puree.
1/2 tsp soaked true saffron, optional.

Simmer for another 1-- 1½ hours until the meat is tender. Taste for seasoning, add salt & pepper as needed.

Venison Stew with Orange and Apricots

2 lb venison stew meat, cut in 1/2" cubes
1 Tb ginger, minced
1 cup onion, 1/2" pieces
1/4 cup coconut oil
2 tsp roasted garlic paste
1/4 cup dry sherry
1/4 cup gluten-free soy sauce or tamari or coconut aminos
6 cups venison (or beef) stock
3 Tb orange marmalade
1 tsp ground star anise seeds
1 cup dried apricots, diced

Saute venison in coconut oil until browned. Remove and reserve.

Saute ginger and onion in remaining oil until brown.

Add garlic paste, sherry, soy sauce, star anise, venison stock, orange marmalade, and dried apricots. Return the venison to the pan. Simmer covered for 3-4 hours until the venison is tender. Stir occasionally to prevent sticking to the bottom of the pan. Add a little water if needed.

Venison Stew with Tomatoes, Onions and Figs

2+ lbs venison stew meat, cut in 1" cubes.
2 onions, chopped coarsely
1/4 cup avocado oil
4 cups tomatoes, chopped coarsely
4 cloves garlic, chopped
1/2 cup parsley, chopped
2 Tb rosemary leaves, minced
1/4 cup raisins
1/2 cup dried figs, chopped
1/2 cup bell or other sweet pepper, 1/2" pieces
1/4 cup ketchup
1/2 tsp thyme
8 cups venison or beef stock
1/2 cup dry white wine
1 tsp salt
1 tsp freshly ground black pepper
1/4 cup coconut roux* to thicken

Brown the venison cubes in avocado oil. Remove and reserve. Brown the onions in the remaining oil. Return the venison to the pot and add the remaining ingredients. Bring to a simmer and cook for 3-4 hours until the venison is tender. Add the roux and heat to thicken. Serve.

Salads

Salade Maison

My standard salad consists of assorted salad greens with other optional vegetables or fruits in a vinaigrette sauce. With the advent of the garden, my (seasonal) options have grown in some ways. On the other hand, living in an isolated Montana community, I do not have the option of visiting the local organic grocer for a few quick purchases.

My garden is likely to yield such salad components as various heirloom lettuces, spinach, mache, wild type arugula, minutina, red orach, stridolo, claytonia, as well as radishes, carrots, chives, tomatoes, apples, and various herbs. Cold-tolerant perennials such as stridolo, minutina, chives, dandelion and self-seeding annuals such as red orach, lamb's quarters and claytonia reward the gardener with early salad greens.

Broccoli is best lightly steamed, and if you peel several inches of stem, you can slice and use those too. I start broccoli inside under lights early. Broccoli with good side shoot production can yield five or six harvests by late October.

Other excellent ingredients which I can't or don't grow include jicama, alfalfa or broccoli sprouts, salted and roasted sunflower seeds, and domestic Agaricus (ie Crimini or button) mushrooms. The references usually recommend against eating wild mushrooms raw, because some toxins are destroyed by cooking, and some people have allergic reactions to wild mushrooms, especially if they are raw.

Use any of the vinaigrette sauces which follow.

I make my own fruit and herb vinegars by steeping fruits or herbs in white wine vinegar for a month or so, then straining them. I ask the local market to order me a case at a time of restaurant supply white wine vinegar, 4 gallons.

Don's Raspberry Vinaigrette Sauce

1/3 cup avocado oil
1/3 cup good olive oil
1/3 cup raspberry vinegar
1 tsp blue poppy seeds
2 tsp Dijon mustard
1 Tb honey
1/2 tsp salt
1/3 tsp black pepper

Combine in a jar with a lid and shake thoroughly or use a hand immersion blender.

For the raspberry vinegar, substitute tarragon wine vinegar or other herb vinegars such as salad burnet vinegar, or chervil vinegar.

Raspberry - Walnut Vinaigrette

1/3 cup avocado oil
1/2 tsp salt
1/3 cup walnut oil (or use all walnut oil)
1/3 cup raspberry vinegar
2 Tb chopped walnuts

1/3 tsp black pepper
1 tsp Dijon mustard
1 Tb honey

Gardener's Herb Salad

Combine

Several lettuces
Spinach
Claytonia leaves (cultivar of miner's lettuce)
Wild type arugula (sylvetta)
Red orach leaves
Apple, diced (1/4 apple per serving)

To these, add small amounts of herbs (like 1 tsp each per serving, chopped): lime or lemon basil leaves (new flowering tops are fine), Thai basil (ditto), chervil, Italian parsley, tarragon, Persian cress, cilantro, etc. according to taste and availability. Most or all of these in combination is the idea. A good garden should have lots of herbs..

Toss with a vinaigrette sauce of your choice.

Avocado Salad Dressing

1 ripe medium avocado, peeled and cut into pieces. Place in the bowl of your food processor.

Add

1/4 cup cultured coconut milk
2 Tb coconut mayonnaise*
1 tsp roasted garlic puree*

1 Tb balsamic vinegar
1 Tb lemon juice
1 tsp salt
1/2 tsp freshly ground black pepper
1 tsp Hot Sweet Chili Garlic Sauce*

Puree. Remove to a container, refrigerate for at least 2 hours.

Makes about one cup.

Add to a green salad and toss. The salad could contain lettuces, spinach, red orach, jicama, radishes, sprouts, various other salad greens, and perhaps also diced cooked chicken breast, smoked salmon or other smoked fish, or lump crab meat.

Cucumber and Pineapple Raita – Style

Normally the Classic Indian salad/ cool side dish, Raita, is made with yoghurt and cucumbers. I use cultured coconut milk in this non-dairy rendering, along with pineapple.

Peel 2 Cucumbers and cut into 1/4" x 1/2-3/4" pieces; salt heavily and let sit for 1 hour. Then squeeze most of the juice out one small handful at a time and add to

2 cups diced fresh pineapple
1 ½ cup cultured coconut milk
1/2 tsp fresh ground coriander
1/4 tsp cardamom powder (its best if you start with whole seeds (not whole pods) and grind them).
1/2 tsp fresh ground roasted cumin
1/4 tsp freshly ground black pepper
2 chopped scallions
1/4 tsp cayenne (optional)

I measure all the spice seeds into my spice grinder and grind 'em all at once. Refrigerate for at least two hours.

Coleslaw

Soak for 1 hour in lightly salted ice water:

>   1 medium head green cabbage or savoy cabbage, shredded
>   1 sweet green pepper, seeded, deribbed and shredded
>   1 sweet onion, finely chopped

Strain through an old dish towel, squeezing all the moisture out. Combine

>   2 cups cider vinegar
>   1 ½ cups xylitol or coconut sugar
>   1 tsp celery seeds
>   2 tsp Dijon-style mustard
>   1 tsp brown mustard seeds
>   1 tsp caraway seeds
>   1 tsp coriander seeds, fresh ground
>   1 tsp blue poppy seeds

Simmer for 20 minutes. Cool. Add the squeezed vegetables plus 1/2 cup grated carrot to the vinegar mixture and refrigerate for 12 hours.

Mom's Upgraded Sweet Potato Salad

Combine

>   1/2 cup finely chopped sweet onion
>   1/2 cup finely chopped celery
>   2 eggs, hard boiled, peeled and mashed

2 Tb xylitol or coconut sugar

1 tsp molasses

1 Tb mayonnaise, preferably homemade coconut mayonnaise*)

2 tsp Dijon style mustard

1 Tb thick coconut milk

1 tsp salt

2 grilled sweet potatoes, blackened skin removed and mashed (1+ lb)

1/2 cup finely chopped pineapple

Refrigerate for 4+ hours.

Serves four.

Sauerkraut and Beet Salad

Combine 3 cups raw live sauerkraut, drained

1 cup baked, shredded beets

1 cup peeled, julienned apple

1/2 cup shredded carrots

1/2 cup diced sweet onion

Mix to combine,

1/4 cup mustard vinaigrette

1/2 tsp salt

1/2 tsp freshly ground black pepper

1 Tb honey

(Optional) 1/4 cup coconut mayonnaise*

Mix together and refrigerate for two or more hours. Serves six.

Broccoli and Roasted Tomato Salad with Tarragon Mustard Vinaigrette

One 6" head broccoli, broken into florettes, and the stems peeled and sliced, and lightly steamed. Cool.

>   2/3 cup roasted tomatoes*, chopped
>   2 scallions, chopped.

Toss with Tarragon-Mustard Vinaigrette.

Vegetables

Fresh Morels

Morels are very subtle in flavor, distinctive and tender and by universal acclaim, delicious. Herbs and spices should be used very sparingly, if at all. Long, slow sauteeing concentrates and enhances the flavor, which becomes intense. When brown, the morels are not as tender, but have more flavor and aroma.

Long, slow-cooked chopped fresh morels make a great start on a fine sauce. Saute with shallots in coconut oil.

Fresh morels can also be sauteed in a batter – I like an egg dip followed by a bread crumb coating. Or they can be battered and deep fried, or stuffed and baked. It is best if they are halved, so as to detect beetles and slugs.

Dried Morels

I prefer to dry morels to preserve them, or make Duxelles. When reconstituted in water, they make an excellent sauce. Save the soaking water and add it to the sauce.

Other Wild Mushrooms

Besides morels, there are many other wild mushrooms that can be found in western Montana and in many other locales in the U.S. Many are world-class. I have identified about 30 different types of edible mushrooms growing in the wild (and in my yard).

The mushrooms I am especially happy to find include the King Bolete (Cepe, Porcini, Steinpilz in Europe). The cepe is usually dried and used in sauces, where it provides a rich mushroom base. Even if I have other mushrooms for a sauce, I will add a few pieces of cepe as well.

Other first rate mushrooms include the golden and white chanterelles, sweet tooths (hedgehog), and hericium (tooth comb). I am also happy to find shrimp russula, fried chicken mushrooms, meadow mushrooms, oyster mushrooms, candy caps, and will pick others as well. Spring agrocybe mushrooms grow in my permaculture beds and yard.

Tip: If you have some older mushrooms, with perhaps some beetle larvae present, as well as stems, you can make a wild mushroom powder which is handy as a quick mushroom addition to soups and sauces. First, slice and dry them (I use big framed screens set in the sun or run a fan across them). As they dry, most of the larvae evacuate the drying mushrooms and fall through the screen to die. When thoroughly dry, grind the slices to a powder in a blender and store in a bottle. I add some dessicant powder packets and peppercorns and bay leaves to dry mushrooms to ward off insects.

Any time you get the idea of going out to look for wild mushrooms, you need at least one good field guide (I have six), and perhaps sign up for a class. Big blond morels are found in Montana cottonwood river bottoms in the spring, along with oyster mushrooms. Oyster mushrooms are also found in the fall in the river bottoms, along with Hericiums tooth combs). Meadow mushrooms are found starting in June in the valleys, frequently around old sheep sheds. Big puffballs can also be found. Fairy rings (Marasmius oriades) sometime grow in lawns, as do other things. I have had cloud ear mushrooms growing in my permaculture, and meadow mushrooms and Agrocybe praecox (spring agrocybe) in my yard and permaculture.

For the most part, the rest of the wild mushrooms are found in the mountains, mostly from July on into the fall. Black/ brown morels can be found coming up the first year or two after a forest fire, starting in June.

In Montana, climate is variable, and adequate rain along with warm temperatures are required for a good mushroom crop. It doesn't always happen.

Accurate identification is essential. There are poisonous mushrooms around which can be confused with edible mushrooms. Some will make you sick, others will kill you. There are hundreds of different mushrooms growing in Montana, as elsewhere, and many have never been scientifically described or tested for edibility. You can find mushrooms which smell good and appear to be possibly edible, but unless you can say for sure what it is, you will have to pass.

Morel Duxelles

An excellent way to save morels (or other wild mushrooms), ready to go into a sauce or stuffing.

> 1 lb fresh morels, finely minced.
> 3-4 Tb coconut oil
> 2 Tb minced scallions or shallots
> 1/2 tsp salt
> 1/2 tsp freshly ground white pepper
> 2 Tb gluten-free flour
> 1/2 cup dry white wine
> 1/2 cup thick coconut milk (canned)

Saute the scallions or shallots for a minute in the coconut oil until they begin to brown,, then add the minced morels and saute on fairly high heat for several minutes until the morels begin to brown and separate, then add the salt and pepper and flour, and cook over moderate heat, stirring, for 2 minutes.

Add the wine and mix then add the coconut milk and boil to reduce and thicken. Taste for seasoning.

This recipe would also work for other kinds of mushrooms. Freeze in small jars.

Braised Mushrooms

Serve this as a vegetable side dish over rice, or as a topping for an omelet.

2 cups fresh mushrooms, sliced, or use 1 cup dried mushrooms. Any number of mushrooms would be good in this dish, including meadow mushrooms, slippery jack boletes or cêpes, chanterelles, sweet tooths, fried chicken mushrooms, shrimp russula, spring agrocybe, oyster mushrooms, morels, or use supermarket crimini mushrooms.
1 onion, diced
3-4 cloves garlic, minced
2 Tb Madeira wine
3 Tb coconut oil
1/2 tsp rubbed sage
1/2 tsp freshly ground caraway seeds
1/4 tsp freshly ground black pepper
1 ½ cup dried mushroom soaking water and/or vegetable or chicken stock
1/2 tsp salt

Sauté onions and garlic in coconut oil. If using soaked dried mushrooms, squeeze out the water and toss with the onions and garlic and sauté for 1-2 minutes. If using fresh mushrooms, remove the onions and garlic and set aside, add more oil as needed, and sauté the mushrooms until lightly browned. Combine the mushrooms, onions and garlic with the Madeira, stock, and spices. Simmer for 15-20 minutes, then thicken with 1 tsp arrowroot dissolved in 1 Tb water.

Maple Syrup and Mustard Sauce for Broccoli

2Tb maple syrup
2 tsp Dijon style mustard
1/4 tsp freshly ground black pepper
1/2 tsp salt
2 Tb coconut oil

Combine and melt together, pour over lightly steamed broccoli florets and peeled, sliced stems.

Coconut Yoghurt – Mustard Sauce for Steamed Broccoli

1/2 cup cultured coconut milk
2 tsp honey
2 tsp hot Chinese prepared mustard
2 Tb gluten free black soy sauce or tamari

Mix, heat briefly to warm, and pour over 1/2 lb steamed broccoli and stir to mix. Serves four.

Steamed Broccoli and Carrots with Sweet Chili Sauce

4 cups broccoli florets
2 cups carrots, julienned
2 Tb coconut oil
1/4 cup Hot Sweet Chili Garlic Sauce*
2 Tb gluten-free tamari, soy sauce, or coconut aminos

Steam the carrots for 5 minutes, then add the broccoli and steam another 5 minutes. Combine the coconut oil, chili sauce, and tamari sauce and serve with the cooked broccoli and carrots.

Baked Spaghetti Squash with Basil and Maple Syrup

Cover with aluminum foil and bake spaghetti squash about 1 hour at 350 degrees. Cut in half and scoop out** the seeds. Then shred the flesh with a fork and toss with

> 1/3 cup coconut oil,
> 1 tsp minced ginger sautéed in the coconut oil
> 2/3 cup chopped fresh basil (or 1/4 cup frozen parboiled basil)
> 1/4 cup maple syrup
> 1/2 tsp salt
> Heat together for 10 minutes on low heat, covered.

I made some handy spoon knives, ground to an edge on a grinder, with antler handles, which are great for hollowing out vegetables. I made various sizes. **If you make your own, be sure you label them clearly and keep away from children! I made little scabbards out of leather for them.

Apples, Onions, and Bananas in Sweet Red Curry Sauce

> 1/2 cup chopped onions
> 2 tsp chopped ginger
> 1 chopped garlic clove
> Saute 3-4 minutes in 1 Tb coconut oil,

Then add

> 1 large diced apple
> 1 Tb Thai style red curry powder

Saute on medium heat for 10 minutes, stirring regularly, then add

> 1/4 cup water
> 1 diced ripe banana
> 1/4 cup cultured coconut milk
> 1 Tb xylitol or coconut sugar
> 1 tsp salt

Bring to a simmer for 2-3 minutes. Serves two.

Basic Stir-Fried Vegetables

> To serve 3-4
> 1 pound vegetables**
> 3 slices fresh ginger root
> 1 clove garlic, minced or 1-2 scallions, chopped
> 1/2 cup stock (chicken or vegetable)
> 1 Tb dark soy sauce, tamari sauce, or coconut aminos
> 2 tsp dry sherry wine
> 1 tsp xylitol or coconut sugar
> 2 Tb avocado or grapeseed oil
> 1/2 tsp salt

Prepare vegetables** by slicing in bite-sized pieces. (They may be cooked individually or in combination.) Mince ginger root and garlic and chop scallions.

Combine stock, soy sauce and sugar.

Heat oil in a wok. A wok is a good thing to own – it is best for this and works for all sorts of cooking tasks.

Add salt, then ginger root and garlic and/ or scallions, and stir-fry a few times. Add vegetables and stir-fry to coat with oil and heat through.

Tougher veggies such as carrots or green beans should be stir-fried for a few minutes, until partially cooked.

Tougher veggies may be parboiled. Tender veggies such as snow peas or broccoli need only a short stir-fry.

Add stock-soy mixture and heat quickly. Then simmer, covered, over medium heat until vegetables are done, tender but still crunchy. (3-4 minutes typically.)

The sauce can be thickened as needed with 1 tsp cornstarch or arrowroot mixed with 1 Tb water.

**Vegetables which work well in a stir-fry include snow peas, sugar snap peas, summer squashes (zucchini), green beans, asparagus, pak (bok) choi, napa (Chinese) cabbage, broccoli, carrots, mushrooms (especially shitake), peas, peppers, spinach, Swiss chard, mung bean sprouts, non-GMO soy bean sprouts, red orach, lamb's quarters, and any number of others. Bamboo shoots and waterchestnuts can be used if you don't mind eating garbage from China. I like to serve stir-fries on a bed of rice.

Meat, such as chicken breast, can be added to a vegetable stir-fry. Cut into boneless bite-size pieces; coat with (for 1/2 lb meat):

    1 Tb cornstarch or arrowroot
    1 Tb soy sauce
    1 tsp dry sherry
    1/2 tsp salt

Marinate for 20 min. or so then stir-fry in oil until the pink is gone. Remove the meat, add more oil as needed, and stir-fry the vegetables. Return the meat to the pan, add the soy sauce mixture (more stock as needed), and simmer 4 minutes or so. Thicken with arrowroot or cornstarch as needed.

Carrots in Vanilla Sauce

1 ½ lb carrots, slice 1/4 inch thick and cook until just tender (12-15 minutes) in just enough filtered water to cover. Remove carrots when tender and reduce cooking broth to about one cup.

Add 1/2 cup coconut sugar or turbinado sugar.

Cook, stirring, until the water has evaporated and big bubbles begin to form and it starts to caramelize. Then add 1/4 cup coconut oil and

1 Tb vanilla extract
1/3 tsp salt
1/4 tsp cinnamon
1/8 tsp fresh ground nutmeg
1/4 tsp cardamom

Return carrots to the pot to mix and reheat. Serves four.

Braised Lettuce with Onions, Apples, Raisins, Celery

Saute in 2 Tb coconut oil until beginning to brown:

1 small onion, chopped
1/2 cup chopped celery

2 cloves garlic, chopped
1 cooking apple, chopped

Add 1 head mature lettuce, chopped
Stir-fry briefly, then add

2 tsp raisins steeped in brandy
2 tsp soaking brandy
1/4 cup Madeira wine
2 cups good brown beef stock
1/2 tsp freshly ground coriander seed powder
1/2 tsp salt
1/2 tsp black pepper
The raisins and brandy

Simmer, partially covered for 40 minutes. Thicken with 1 tsp arrowroot dissolved in 1 Tb water.

Broccoli and Vegetables Stir-fried with Mediterranean Flavors

1 Tb olive oil
2 Tb coconut oil
1 medium onion, chopped
1 cup carrots, julienned
1/2 cup sliced dried mushrooms, reconstituted (save the water)
1 head broccoli cut into florets, stems peeled and sliced
1/2 cup roasted tomatoes*, diced
1 tsp roasted garlic puree*
1/4 cup good pitted black olives, chopped
2 Tb basil, chopped
1 tsp oregano, chopped
1 tsp coconut sugar
1/2 cup water or stock

Brown the onions in the oils. Stir-fry the onions for 3-4 minutes, then add the broccoli and mushrooms and stir-fry for 2 minutes.

Add tomatoes, roasted garlic puree, herbs, sugar and olives, 1/2 cup soaking water or stock, cover and simmer/ steam 3-4 minutes. Thicken with 1/2 tsp dissolved arrowroot. Salt & pepper to taste.

Corn on the Cob

6 ears of corn in the husk
4 Tb coconut oil
1 tsp chipotle pepper powder
1 tsp ancho chili pepper powder
1/2 tsp roasted garlic puree*
1 tsp salt
1 tsp freshly ground black pepper

Grill the corn until the outer husks are mostly black, about 1/2 hour at 400 degrees over direct flame or live coals. (Or place the corn in the coals of a campfire.) Peel and brush with melted coconut oil combined with the spices and salt. Rubber gloves help husk the hot corn. Cut off the top 1" or so and have at it. Put the charred husks in the compost.

If you would like your corn without the spices, just combine coconut oil with salt and pepper and brush it on after the corn is cooked.

Corn 'n Carrots

10 oz frozen or fresh corn kernels
1 large carrot, diced
2 Tb coconut sugar or xylitol plus 1 tsp organic molasses

2 Tb tomato salsa*

1 tsp roasted, ground chili pepper such as ancho; include some chipotle for more heat

1/2 tsp salt

1/4 tsp freshly ground black pepper

Cook carrots and corn in 1/2 cup water, covered, until done, about 10 minutes.

Drain.

Add salsa, sugar, chili, pepper and salt. Simmer 2 min.

Serves four.

Curried Lamb's Quarters or Orach

1+ pint lamb's quarter leaves or red orach leaves

1 shallot or scallion, chopped

Saute in

1 Tb coconut oil

1 Tb olive oil

For 3-4 minutes, then add

1 Tb Madras curry powder or curry powder of your choice and saute 30 seconds, then add the lamb's quarters and saute/ stir-fry for 3-4 minutes then add 2 Tb chicken stock or veggie stock + 2 Tb thin coconut milk

Salt to taste and cover, simmer 3-4 minutes

Thicken with 1 tsp arrowroot dissolved in 1 Tb water.

Lamb's quarters (also called pigweed) is a common weed that grows in my yard and as a weed in my garden, and is widely distributed. Commonly found in barnyards. It is one of the earliest greens available for harvest in the spring.

Red orach, another early green (although it is red) can be added to this dish along with the lamb's quarters, or substituted. Orach comes in other colors also. Substitute spinach leaves.

Dairy-Free Pizza Topping

For one 14" pizza. Prepare gluten-free pizza mix or recipe of your choice, mixed, placed on the pan, and pre-baked at 450 degrees for 10 minutes.

Tomato-pepper-mushroom sauce

> 2 Tb olive oil
> 1 cup chopped onion
> 2 cups sliced mushrooms (crimini, meadow mushrooms, spring
>   agrocybe are good choices)
> 1/2 tsp salt
> 1/2 tsp pepper
> 1 cup Tomato-Pepper Omelet Topping
> 1/4 cup chopped calamata olives, or other good black olives
> 1/4 cup water

Saute the onions in the olive oil until translucent. Add the mushrooms and cook until they and the onions begin to brown. Add the tomato-pepper topping and water. Heat to the simmer and stir to combine. Set aside.

Dairy-free coconut-cashew topping (cheese substitute)

> 1/2 cup raw cashew butter
> 1/2 cup thick coconut milk

1 Tb coconut oil (melted)
1 Tb olive oil
2 Tb water

Combine and mix well. It should be easily spreadable. Spread the tomato-pepper-mushroom sauce on the pre-baked dough. Optional: top with sausage slices to taste. Spread the coconut- cashew topping on top. Bake at 450 degrees for 15 minutes.

Puree of Potatoes and Kale

1 ½ lbs potatoes, peeled, boiled 'til tender, drained and reserved.
3-4 cups finely chopped kale sautéed in
1/3 cup coconut oil

with

5 cloves chopped garlic
(or use 1 Tb roasted garlic puree added after the kale is cooked)

For 5 minutes, add

1 cup thin coconut milk
2 tsp salt
1 tsp freshly ground black pepper

Simmer for 5 minutes more, covered. Cool and puree in a blender.

Combine and mash with the potatoes and reheat to serve.

Serves six.

End-of-Winter Curry

Using garden vegetables that were in cold storage or were precooked and frozen.

> 2 lb potatoes cut in ~3/4" pieces
> 1 lb carrots cut in 1/3" slices or bite-size pieces
> 1 cup sauteed, frozen sweet peppers, diced
> 1/3 cup sauteed and frozen serrano peppers or other hot pepper, diced.
> 2 onions, diced
> 1 Tb roasted garlic puree*
> 1 cup roasted tomatoes,*
> 1 Tb minced ginger
> 1/4 + cup coconut oil

Saute the ginger and onions in coconut oil until brown. Remove.

Saute the potatoes and carrots until brown. (Add more coconut oil if needed.)

Combine peppers, tomatoes, and garlic with the potatoes, carrots, and onions.

Add

> 2 ½ cups vegetable stock or chicken stock
> 1 tsp tumeric
> 1 Tb roasted cumin, half ground, half whole.
> 1 Tb fresh ground coriander
> 1/2 tsp black pepper
> 1 Tb ground ancho chili
> 1 tsp garam masala spice mixture
> 1 tsp salt

Simmer for 1/2 hour or until potatoes and carrots are tender.

Add

> 1 cup cultured coconut milk
> 1/2 cup chopped cilantro.

Bring back to a simmer and serve. 8 servings.

Fava Beans with Black Seed and Roasted Tomatoes

2 cups dry fava beans (also known as broad beans) or use 2 cups fresh beans or frozen beans.

Soak overnight and cut along one side and peel the skin off. Simmer partially covered for 30-35 minutes until tender. Drain. If using fresh young beans, simmer for 5 minutes or until tender, drain and cool, then peel.

Saute 2 tsp black seed (black onion seed, kalonji, Nigella sativa) in 2 Tb coconut oil for 30 seconds, add 1 tsp tumeric and cook another 30 seconds, stirring, and add

> 1/2 cup roasted tomatoes*, chopped
> 2 tsp roasted garlic puree*
> 1/2 cup fresh basil, chopped
> 1/2 cup water

The drained fava beans

> 1/2 tsp salt

Simmer together for 10 minutes then serve.

You could substitute lima beans in this recipe. One source said some people react to fava beans, particularly those of Mediterranean heritage.

Fused Eggplant

> 3 long oriental eggplants, sliced 1/2"

Coat eggplants with

> 1 tsp fresh ground coriander seed
> 1 tsp fresh ground roasted cumin*
> 1 tsp cayenne
> 1/2 tsp salt
> 1/2 tsp pepper
> 1 Tb granulated onion
> 1 tsp granulated garlic
> 1 Tb almond flour
> 2 tsp minced fresh ginger
> 1/3 cup coconut oil

Saute eggplants and ginger in coconut oil until brown.

Add

> 1 tsp roasted garlic puree*
> 1/2 cup plain cultured coconut milk
> 1 cup thick coconut milk (canned)

Simmer 10 minutes. Serves four.

Orange Pistachio Asparagus

1 lb asparagus, peeled and cut in 1/2" sections
1 quarter-sized slice ginger, minced
1 Tb dried orange peel, rehydrated and shredded (save the soaking
    water) or use fresh orange zest
1/2 + cup toasted salted pistachios (not dyed), coarsely chopped
2 Tb coconut oil
1/4 tsp orange oil
1/4 tsp salt
1/4 tsp black pepper

Stir-fry ginger and orange peel briefly in coconut oil then add asparagus and stir-fry briefly, then add 1/4 cup of the orange peel soaking water + orange oil, salt, and pepper.

Cook for 3-4 min, stirring, as the liquid boils down. Add pistachios.

Serves six.

Puree of Potatoes, Onions, Corn and Peppers

4 cups potatoes, peeled and parboiled
4 ears of corn, grilled in their husks (about 3 cups)
1 cup onions, chopped
1/4 cup coconut oil
2 tsp roasted garlic puree*
1 cup (red) bell or sweet peppers, minced
1 tsp salt
1/2 tsp freshly ground black pepper
2 Tb Italian parsley, minced

Parboil the potatoes until tender, drain and set aside. Dice coarsely.

Cut the cooked kernels of corn from the ears. Chop lightly in the food processor, leaving partial kernels.

Saute the onions in 2 Tb coconut oil until lightly browned. Set aside.

Saute the peppers in another 2 Tb coconut oil until well done. Set aside.

Combine the potatoes, parsley, onion and roasted garlic with salt and pepper and the coconut oil used to saute the onions. Puree in a food processor. Fold in the minced sauteed peppers with their cooking oil, and the corn kernels.

Form into patties and brown lightly in coconut oil.

Serves six.

Pureed Roasted Sweet Potatoes, Beets and Onions

3 sweet potatoes
2 cups onion, chopped
1 clove garlic, chopped
1/4 cup coconut oil
3 medium large beets

Roast sweet potatoes on the grill until the skin is mostly black and the inside is mushy. Scoop out the pulp and donate the blackened skins to the compost.

Saute chopped onion and garlic until brown in the coconut oil.

Bake beets in an oiled casserole, covered, at 350 degrees until done, about 1 ½ hours. Cool enough to peel and chop.

Add to the food processor along with the onion, garlic, coconut oil and sweet potato pulp.

Add 2 Tb walnut oil

    1/2 tsp freshly ground black pepper
    1 tsp salt
    1/4 tsp freshly grated nutmeg
    1/2 tsp ground dry ginger
    2 Tb raspberry vinegar
    2-4 Tb water

Combine and puree. Taste for seasonings. Simmer for 10-15 minutes. Serve hot.

Quinoa with Roasted Tomatoes and Peppers

Saute

    1 chopped scallion in
    2 Tb coconut oil

Add

    1 cup quinoa
    2 cups chicken stock or vegetable stock
    1/4 cup chopped roasted tomatoes
    1 Tb chopped fresh basil
    1/2 tsp roasted garlic puree
    1 Tb chopped Italian parsley
    1/2 cup red bell pepper or sweet Italian pepper, chopped

1/2 tsp salt, or to taste
1/2 tsp freshly ground black pepper

Bring to a boil and simmer covered for 15 minutes or until liquid is absorbed. Let sit for 5 minutes, stir to fluff.

Riced Cauliflower Curry

Rice 1 large cauliflower using the grating blade on the food processor.

2 Tb ginger, finely chopped
8 cloves garlic, finely chopped
2+ hot fresh peppers, chopped
1 yellow onion, chopped
2 Tb coconut oil
2 Tb avocado oil

Stir-fry ginger, garlic, peppers, onions until onion is translucent, about 10 min. Add cauliflower and mix.

Add

1 Tb freshly ground coriander
2 tsp cumin seeds, roasted then ground
2 tsp garam masala spice mix
1 tsp tumeric
2 tsp salt
2 Tb lemon juice
1/2 cup tomato sauce
1 cup water
1/3 cup chopped cilantro

Cook gently for 15-20 min, covered, until cauliflower is done. Add chopped cilantro and mix. Serves six.

Roasted Sweet Potato, Beet, and Cherry Puree

Roast 4 sweet potatoes on the grill until blackened (and cooked through); cool enough to skin. Scoop out the soft pulp and reserve.

Mince and sauté

   3 shallots in
   1/3 cup coconut oil. Reserve.

Roast 3 large beets in a covered casserole at 350 degrees until done (about an hour) Then cool and skin, and chop.

Simmer 2 cups fresh or frozen pitted cherries in 1/3 cup Marsala wine for 5 minutes.

Then add

   1 Tb balsamic vinegar
   1/2 tsp freshly ground black pepper
   1/4 tsp cardamom
   2 tsp salt

The reserved sweet potatoes, shallots and oil, and beets. Puree it all together in a food processor. Reheat to serve.

Snow Peas, Carrots and Pineapple in Basil Coconut Sauce

Combine

> 1/2 can coconut milk
> 1/4 c. Madeira wine
> 1/2 cup water
> 2 tsp (lemon) curry powder
> 1 tsp salt

Simmer 6-8 minutes,stirring, to reduce.

> 4 cups snow peas, de-stringed
> 2 cups carrots, 1/2" slices
> 2 cups pineapple, 1/2" chunks
> 1/2 cup chopped fresh basil

Then add the carrots and cook 3-4 min.

Then add the pineapple and cook 2-3 min.

Then add the snow peas and basil and cook 3-4 minutes.

Serves 4-6. I would recommend serving it on a bed of rice.

Sweet and Sour Rhubarb and Pineapple

Sauté

> 2 slices ginger, minced
> 2 scallions, minced

in

  2 Tb coconut oil for 1 minute

Add

  4 cups rhubarb, 1/2" sections
  2 cups fresh pineapple, 1/2" sections

Stir-fry briefly then add

  2 Tb gluten-free dark soy sauce, tamari, or coconut aminos
  1 Tb dry sherry
  1/4 cup coconut sugar or xylitol
  1/4 cup Balsamic vinegar

Cook 6-8 minutes

Dissolve 2 tsp cornstarch or arrowroot in 1 Tb water and stir in to thicken for 1 minute.

Stir-fried Indian-Spiced Zucchini, Potatoes, Peppers and Mangoes

  4 cups zucchini, 1/2" – 3/4" dice
  3 cups potatoes, parboiled
  1 bell pepper, sliced
  1/2 cup fresh serrano or other hot peppers, diced
  2 cups tomatoes, chopped
  1/2 cup dried mangoes, 1/2" dice, soaked in 1 cup water
  1 cup snow peas, strings removed
  1 cup thick coconut milk (canned)
  1 onion, chopped
  1 tsp roasted garlic
  1 tsp salt

1 tsp black pepper, ground
2 tsp cumin seeds, freshly roasted and then ground
1 tsp turmeric
2 tsp freshly ground coriander
2 tsp garam masala spice mix
1/2 cup basil, chopped
1 tsp cayenne (optional)
1 Tb fresh ginger, minced
3 Tb avocado oil
1 Tb coconut oil

Parboil the potatoes until just tender. Dice 1/2"- 3/4". Reserve.

Prepare all the vegetables and have them ready to cook.

In a wok, heat the oil and saute the ginger for 1 minute on high heat. Add the onions and stir-fry for 4 minutes, then add the peppers and stir-fry another 4 minutes. Then add the zucchini and snow peas and stir-fry for 2 minutes.

Add the tomatoes, mangoes with soaking water, potatoes, coconut milk, roasted garlic, salt, black pepper, cumin, tumeric, coriander, garam masala, basil and cayenne. Bring to a simmer and cook for 10 minutes, covered.

Serves six.

Stir-fried Lamb's Quarters and Carrots in Black Bean Sauce

4 cups lamb's quarter leaves (or substitute bite-sized pieces of kale leaves, red orach or spinach, or broccoli)
1 ½ cups julienned or grated carrots
1/2 cup sliced bell or sweet Italian peppers in bite-sized pieces

1/4 + cup diced serrano or jalapeno peppers

1 scallion, sliced

2 Tb avocado oil, 2 Tb coconut oil

1/2 tsp salt

1 Tb fresh ginger, minced

2 Tb fermented black beans, soaked for 2 hours in filtered water,
   then drained and mashed to a pulp

1 tsp roasted garlic puree (or 2 garlic cloves, minced)

1 tsp xylitol or coconut sugar

2 Tb gluten- free soy sauce, tamari sauce, or coconut aminos

1 Tb dry sherry

1/2 cup water

1/2 tsp arrowroot dissolved in 2 tsp water

1 tsp toasted sesame oil

Heat the oil on high heat with the salt and add the ginger, cook for a minute, add the black beans, then add the carrots, peppers, and scallion. Stir-fry until the carrots and peppers are beginning to be tender and cooked. Add the garlic and lamb's quarter leaves and stir-fry for a couple of minutes. Then add the xylitol, soy sauce, sherry and water. Cover and simmer for 4 minutes, then thicken with arrowroot (or cornstarch), remove from the heat and mix in the sesame oil. Serve over rice. Serves 3-4 with other dishes.

Tangerine Sauce for Sugar Snap Peas or Asparagus

2 Tb chopped shallots

2 Tb coconut oil

1 Tb walnut oil

1+ Tb tangerine peel (zest). Soak first if dry and save the water.

1/4 cup chopped pecans (or pistachios)

Saute shallots in the oils for 2 minutes on moderate heat.

Add the chopped tangerine peel and sauté until tangerine peel and shallot are lightly browned, 3-4 minutes.

Add nuts and sauté 1 minute

Add

> Juice from 1 tangerine (or 10 drops tangerine oil)
> 1/4 cup white wine (if using oil instead of juice, increase wine to 1/2 cup
> and also add the soaking water).

Reduce by half. Makes a mild and savory sauce. Salt & pepper to taste

Optional- For more kick, add 1 Tb Hot Sweet Chili Garlic Sauce*.

Pour over 3 cups boiled sugar snap peas or snow peas (strings removed), cooked until just tender or baked or steamed or baked peeled asparagus. Good also served over fish.

Stir-fried Pak Choi, Carrots, Dates, and Pineapple in Tarragon Coconut Sauce

> 1 Tb coconut oil
> 1 Tb avocado oil
> 1/2 tsp salt
> 1 Tb minced fresh ginger
> 2 scallions, diced
> 1 ½ cup julienned carrots
> 2 Tb diced fresh red serrano peppers or other hot red pepper
> 4 cups sliced pak choi
> 1 ½ cup fresh pineapple, 1/2" dice
> 1/4 cup minced fresh tarragon
> 1/2 cup diced dates
> 1 Tb gluten-free tamari sauce, soy sauce or coconut aminos

2 Tb Madeira wine
1 cup thick canned coconut milk
1/2 tsp ground star anise seeds

Heat the salt in the oils and saute the ginger for 1 minute, add the scallions and cook for another minute, then add the carrots and stir-fry for 4 minutes.

Then add the peppers and pak choi stems and stir-fry for 2 minutes, add chopped pak choi leaves and stir-fry another minute, then add the pineapple, dates, and tarragon and stir-fry another minute.

Then add the tamari, Madeira, coconut milk and star anise. Simmer for 3-4 minutes, then add 1/2 tsp arrowroot dissolved in a bit of water, and cook to thicken. Serves six, over rice.

Wild Rice Casserole

Thoroughly wash 1 cup wild rice

Saute

> 1 medium onion, chopped, in
> 1 Tb coconut oil until lightly browned.

If you have fresh wild mushrooms, cut in 1/2" cubes to make 1 cup, saute with the onions, or add 1/2 cup dried wild mushrooms, soaked and cut in 1/2" cubes to the onions as they finish browning. In a pinch you could use fresh organic crimini mushrooms from the store, enriched with 1 Tb cepes, finely chopped or powdered.

Add

> 1/2 cup chopped celery
> 1 tsp roasted garlic, or saute 2 cloves chopped garlic with the onions.

Add 4 cups water or chicken stock or vegetable stock and bring to
a boil and simmer 40 minutes, or until tender.
Fluff and add 1/2 cup chopped roasted pecans.

Serves four.

Stir-fried Vegetables with Hot Sweet Black Bean Sauce

3 Tb avocado oil
1 Tb coconut oil
1 tsp salt
2 tsp minced fresh ginger
3 garlic cloves, minced
2 Tb fermented dried black beans, soaked for 2 hours in water,
drained and mashed with the garlic
8-12 deseeded dried hot peppers
1 onion, diced
2 cups broccoli florets and peeled stem slices
3 cups mushrooms, sliced (I originally made this dish with Spring
agrocybe mushrooms from my permaculture beds. You could
use crimini mushrooms, meadow mushrooms, or oyster
mushrooms.)
4 cups snow peas, string removed
1 cup pineapple, 1/2" dice
1/2 cup roasted cashews, halved
2 Tb Hot Sweet Chili Garlic Sauce*
1 Tb dry sherry
2 Tb gluten-free tamari, soy sauce, or coconut aminos
1 cup water or mushroom soaking liquid
2 tsp arrowroot dissolved in 1 Tb water
1 Tb toasted sesame oil

Optional: you could include diced zucchini, sliced pak choi or napa cabbage, fresh sweet and/or hot peppers, or sliced carrots.

Prepare the vegetables and have ready to cook. Drain the black beans and mash in a mortar with the garlic.

Heat the oil with the salt in a wok. Add the ginger and peppers and cook for a minute. Then add the black bean garlic mixture and cook for another minute. Then add the onion and cook for 3-4 minutes or until tender.

Then add the mushrooms and stir-fry for several minutes until beginning to brown. Add the snow peas and broccoli and stir-fry for 2-3 minutes. Add the pineapple, Hot Sweet Chili Garlic Sauce, tamari and sherry, and the water. Cover and bring to a simmer, cook for 3-4 minutes, stirring once or twice. Uncover and add the arrowroot and cashews. Cook until the sauce is thickened. Serves six to eight.

Stir-Fried Vegetables with Indian Flavorings

2 Tb coconut oil
2 Tb avocado oil
8-12 seeded hot red peppers
1 Tb finely minced fresh ginger
1 tsp turmeric
1 cup onion, chopped
1/2 cup fresh serrano or jalapeno peppers, sliced
1 cup fresh bell or other sweet peppers, sliced
1/2 cup garlic scapes, if available, or substitute 3 cloves garlic, minced
1 cup crimini or meadow mushrooms, sliced
2 cups zucchini in 1/2" cubes
1/2 tsp salt

2 tsp roasted cumin seeds, ground
2 tsp fresh-ground coriander seeds
2 tsp cayenne powder
1/2 tsp freshly ground black pepper
2 tsp garam masala spice mix
2 Tb ketchup
1/2 cup roasted tomatoes), chopped or 2/3 cup tomato sauce
1/2 cup thick canned coconut milk
1 cup water or vegetable stock

Optional:

1 cup carrots, julienned

Heat the oils, add the salt and the dry hot peppers. Fry for 2-3 minutes, then add the ginger and turmeric and fry for a minute, then add the onion and stir-fry for 4-5 minutes, then add the hot and sweet peppers and garlic and stir-fry for 2-3 minutes, then add the mushrooms and fry for a couple of minutes, then add the zucchini, napa cabbage and snow peas and fry for 2-3 minutes.

Add the turmeric, cumin, coriander, and cayenne. Stir-fry for a minute, then add the ketchup, tomatoes, coconut milk, water or stock, and garam masala.

Cover and cook over medium low for 4 minutes. Thicken with 2 tsp arrowroot dissolved in 1 Tb water. Serves 6-8.

Thai-Chinese Green Curry Stir-fried Vegetables

1 Tb coconut oil
1 cup canned coconut milk
3 Tb fish sauce

1 Tb xylitol or coconut sugar

1 Tb lime juice

3 Tb green curry paste (available in oriental grocery stores, or get a Thai cookbook and make your own)

3 cups snow peas, string removed

4 cups zucchini, chopped

4 cups napa cabbage or pak choi, sliced

2 cups pineapple, diced

2 Tb coconut oil

2 Tb ginger, minced

1 cup onion, diced

3 garlic cloves, minced

1/2 cup serrano or jalapeno pepper, diced

1/4 cup chopped cilantro leaves

Combine 1 Tb coconut oil, coconut milk, fish sauce, xylitol, lime juice and green curry paste and simmer for 20 minutes to reduce, stirring. Set aside.

Heat 2 Tb coconut oil in a wok and stir fry the ginger for 1 minute.

Add the onion, peppers, and garlic and cook until the onions are translucent.

Add the zucchini, napa cabbage and snow peas and stir-fry for 3-4 minutes.

Add the pineapple and reserved curry mixture. Bring to a boil, reduce heat to low, cover, and simmer for 3-4 minutes. Fold in the cilantro and cook for 1 minute. Serves six.

Thai-Chinese Fusion Stir-fried Vegetables with Hot Sweet Basil Coconut Sauce

For a good wok full, enough to serve 5-6 people, 6-8 cups of vegetables.

Choose from among: snow peas, zucchini, carrots, peppers, beans, pineapple, Chinese cabbage, pac choi, as well as bamboo shoots and waterchestnuts if you don't mind the idea of eating food from China and SE Asia... I avoid it because of sanitation issues.

Stir-fry in the usual manner, giving carrots and peppers more time than some of the others.

    3 slices ginger root, minced
    2 cloves garlic, minced
    2 scallions, Cut in 1/2" sections
    1 tsp salt

Fry in 3 Tb coconut oil-- add the salt to the oil, then starting with the ginger, then the garlic and scallions, then add the carrots, peppers, beans and proceed to stir-fry for 4 minutes, then add other ingredients and continue to stir-fry for 3-4 minutes.

Then add

    1 cup thick coconut milk
    1/2 cup chopped basil
    4 Tb Hot Sweet Thai Chili-Garlic Sauce*
    3-4 drops lemongrass essential oil

Bring to a simmer and cook for 3-4 minutes. Then add

    2 tsp arrowroot powder (or organic, non-GMO cornstarch)
        dissolved in 1 Tb water to thicken.

Yellow Curry Zucchini, Pepper and Potato Stir-Fry

Combine

    1 cup thick coconut milk (canned)
    1/4 cup Thai yellow curry paste

Simmer for 15 minutes to reduce, stirring frequently. Reserve.

Parboil until just tender, then drain. Reserve.

    3 cups peeled boiling potatoes, 3/4" dice
    1 Tb coconut oil
    2 Tb avocado oil
    1 Tb minced ginger
    1 medium onion, quartered and sliced
    4 cups zucchini or other summer squash, 1/2" dice
    1 cup bell or other sweet pepper, sliced in bite-sized pieces
    1/3 cup fresh serrano or jalapeno peppers, or hot pepper of your
        choice, either red or green, chopped

Stir-fry the ginger for 1 minute in the oils, then add the onion and stir-fry for 3-4 minutes, then add the zucchini and peppers and stir-fry for 3 minutes.

Add and mix in

    1 cup chopped tomatoes
    1 tsp salt
    1/2 tsp tumeric
    1/2 tsp freshly ground black pepper
    1 tsp roasted garlic puree*
    1/2 cup water or vegetable stock

The reserved potatoes

The coconut milk- curry paste

Simmer covered for 5-6 minutes.

Serves six.

Curried Cucumber with Peanuts and Carrots

3 cucumbers
1 onion, chopped
1 Tb fresh ginger, minced
2 Tb coconut oil
1/2 cup fresh hot peppers, or to taste, chopped
1 cup julienned carrots
1/2 cup roasted tomatoes*, chopped
1/2 cup organic peanuts, chopped, or 1/3 cup crunchy organic peanut butter
2 tsp roasted garlic puree
1 tsp coriander, freshly ground
1 tsp roasted cumin seeds, freshly ground
1/2 tsp black pepper, freshly ground
1/4 tsp cardamom seeds, freshly ground
1 tsp black seed
1 tsp sweet neem leaves (curry leaves)
2 tsp ancho chili powder
1 tsp turmeric
1 tsp garam masala
1 tsp cayenne (optional)
1/2 cup cultured coconut milk
1/2 cup water

Peel the cucumbers and cut into 1/2" X 1" pieces. Salt heavily and let drain 1 hour. Rinse thoroughly with cold water, drain and squeeze as much juice from them as possible, one small handful at a time.

Sauté the onion and ginger in coconut oil until the onion is translucent. Add the hot peppers and carrots and sauté 3-4 minutes.

Add the cucumbers, toss with the onion and ginger for 1 minute, then add roasted tomatoes (or fresh tomatoes), roasted garlic puree, peanuts or peanut butter, coriander, cumin, black pepper, cardamom, black seed, sweet neem, ancho chili powder, turmeric, garam masala and cultured coconut milk.

Simmer for 5 minutes. Serve over rice. Serves 6-8.

Fish & Shellfish

Broiled Halibut with Dried Papaya Sauce

Coat 2 halibut steaks with melted coconut oil, salt and broil; top with this sauce:

To serve two:

Saute

> 1 Tb minced shallot
> 1 tsp chopped fresh ginger

In

> 1 Tb coconut oil

Add

> 2 Tb gluten-free black soy, tamari, or coconut aminos
> 1/2 cup chopped dried papaya
> 1 Tb dry sherry
> 1/2 cup water
> 1 Tb Chinese Plum Sauce
> 1 Tb (black) Chinese vinegar

Simmer 10 minutes and serve.

Crab Stuffing

> 2 cups chopped cooked crab meat
> 1/4 cup chopped shallots, sauteed in
> 1 Tb coconut oil, then add
> 1 ½ cups white wine

1 cup fish stock
1/4 tsp thyme or 1 small sprig
1 Tb fresh tarragon, chopped
1/2 tsp white pepper

Cook down to concentrate the flavor.

Add 1 can thick coconut milk incrementally, boiling down a little at a time. Add salt and pepper to taste.

Add cooked crab to warm.

Can be used to top fish filets or stuff morel mushroom halves prior to baking or it would be excellent over pasta or to stuff crepes.

Optional: Saute crab shells until brown in avocado oil, if you have them. Add water to cover, bring to a boil then simmer for 1+ hours. Strain and discard the shells, then proceed with the recipe.

Optional. 1 cup chopped sauteed mushrooms. Chanterelles, sweet tooths or tooth combs (hericium) or shrimp russula would all be excellent. See also Shrimp Sauce (page).

Crayfish in Coconut Cashew Sauce

Combine and mix thoroughly, preferably with a mixer or hand immersion blender. It should be smooth, free of lumps.

1/3 cup dry white wine
1 Tb cognac or brandy
1/2 cup thick coconut milk
2/3 cup fish/ shellfish stock
1/2 cup raw cashew butter
1/2 tsp sweet paprika

1/2 tsp salt
1/2 tsp freshly ground white pepper

---

1 lb shelled and deveined crayfish tails (or lump crab meat or
   lobster)
2 Tb coconut oil

Heat the oil on high then add the crayfish tails. It may be best to do
it in two batches. Sauté to sear the tails, then remove and reserve.

Add to a sauce pan or small wok:

1 Tb coconut oil
2 shallots, chopped

Sauté for 2 minutes, then add the sauce mixture, above. Simmer for
5 minutes, then add the reserved crayfish tails. Bring to the simmer
again, cover loosely and simmer for 10 minutes.

Stir occasionally, scraping the bottom.

Serves 3-4. Rice is a nice accompaniment.

Crayfish in Coconut Cashew Sauce could be wrapped with crepes
after the initial simmering, topped with sauce, and baked . It could
also be combined with sautéed mushrooms.

Don's Indonesian –
Style Shrimp Brochettes

1 ½ lb large shrimp, peeled and deveined
1 Tb xylitol or coconut sugar
2 tsp molasses

2 cloves garlic, minced

1/2 tsp salt

2 Tb dark soy sauce, tamari, or coconut aminos

1 Tb avocado or grapefruit seed oil

2 tsp freshly ground roasted cumin*

Marinate shrimp with the above ingredients for a few hours.

Thread on skewers and grill over charcoal for a few minutes until just firm.

Serve with Chinese plum sauce or mango chutney and/or Thai hot sweet garlic sauce on the side.

Gingered Trout Filets with Cashews

For two trout (or other fish) filets.

Mix

1/4 cup very finely chopped raw cashews

1 Tb very finely chopped candied dry ginger

1 Tb gluten-free flour

1/2 tsp salt

1/2 tsp freshly ground black pepper

Coat the filets thickly with the cashew mixture.

Sauté

1 Tb chopped shallots

In

2 Tb coconut oil

For 1 minute. Push the shallots to the side of the pan and add the trout filets.

Sauté filets until brown, figuring about 10 minutes per inch of thickness. As the shallots brown, remove them to the serving platter, or mound them on top of a browned filet.

Serves two.

Herb Sauce (Basil or Tarragon or French Sorrel) for Fish

1/4 cup chopped shallots sauteed for a few minutes until lightly browned, in 1 Tb coconut oil.

Add

1 ½ cups dry white wine
1 cup fish stock*
1/2 cup chopped fresh basil or tarragon, or French sorrel
1 Tb lemon juice

Reduce to about 1/2 cup, then strain. Return the sauce base to the pan.

Add 1 ½ cup thick canned coconut milk a little at a time, boiling down each time. It should end up fairly thick, enough to coat a spoon and large bubbles form.

Add

2 Tb chopped fresh tarragon or basil (lime or lemon basil is nice), or French sorrel and
1 tsp dijon mustard and simmer briefly.

Serve with sauteed or broiled fish.

Huckleberry- Basil- Pistachio- Coconut Topping for Broiled Fish Filets

1/4 cup huckleberry jam
1/2 cup coconut oil, melted
1/3 cup fresh basil, chopped or 2 Tb parboiled frozen basil
1/3 cup chopped pistachios

Combine, and place on fish filets shortly before they are finished cooking in the broiler. May also be frozen in individual 2 Tb wax paper/ aluminum foil packets for quick convenient use.

Smoked Salmon - Tarragon Coconut Topping for Fish Filets

1 cup coconut oil
1/2 cup boneless smoked salmon, trout or whitefish*
1 Tb lemon juice
1 tsp sugar
1/4 tsp salt, or to taste
1/2 tsp white pepper
2 Tb chopped fresh tarragon
2 Tb chopped toasted almonds

Chop finely in a food processor and place 1 Tb portions on trout filets shortly before they are finished cooking, whether baked or broiled. Or use to top sauteed filets. Could be used for other fish as well.

Orange Tarragon Pistachio Topping
to serve with broiled fish

Briefly sauté

2 chopped scallions or shallots in
1/4 cup coconut oil

Add

1/3 cup chopped pistachios
1 Tb minced orange zest, soaked if dried
8 drops orange oil
2 Tb fresh tarragon, chopped
1/2 tsp salt
2 tsp honey
2 tsp lemon juice
1/2 tsp freshly ground white pepper

Heat 2-3 minutes to combine and spoon over sautéed or broiled fish filets.

One option is to place on fish near the end of cooking, otherwise, simply top the filets as they are served. Incidentally, I do not favor the currently fashionable practice of drizzling a little sauce on a plate, then placing the entrée on top. Serves four.

This can be frozen in individual 2 Tb packets. (I like to wrap in wax paper, then wrap that with aluminum foil, put in a baggie and label.)

Traditionally one would use butter for this sort of thing; I use coconut oil. You could also use coconut manna. Combine the ingredients and freeze in individual single-serving size wax paper/ aluminum foil packets in a labeled baggie. Top the meat with the topping just before cooking is finished, to allow for melting.

Lemon (zest, juice), dill, minced pecan, coconut oil (fish)

Smoked salmon, lemon, dill, coconut oil (fish)

Smoked salmon, tarragon, scallions, pistachio nuts, coconut oil (fish)

Huckleberry, almond, lemon (salmon)

Key lime juice, coconut cream or coconut manna, dark rum, coconut oil, topped with toasted coconut (fish)

Coconut oil- sautéed scallions, tarragon, reduced white wine (fish)

Mushroom Duxelle Coconut Cream Sauce for Fish

Sauté two fish filets in

> 2 Tb coconut oil
> 1 Tb avocado oil

Deglaze the frying pan with

  1/4 cup thick coconut milk
  1/4 cup mushroom Duxelles*
  1/2 cup fish stock

Simmer, stirring, until the sauce reduces and thickens. Serves two.

Pecan Sauce for SautJed Trout

Sauté

  2 chopped scallions or shallots
  2 cloves chopped garlic

in

  2 Tb coconut oil until just beginning to brown.

add

  1 Tb lemon juice, 1 tsp lemon zest
  1 Tb lime juice, 1 tsp lime zest
  1 Tb chopped lime basil
  1/2 cup chopped pecans
  1 Tb honey
  1 tsp salt
  1 tsp fresh ground black pepper
  1/4 cup white wine

Simmer for 5-6 minutes.

Spoon over sautéed trout filets. Two servings.

Pistachio Lime Basil Sauce for Sauteed Trout

Saute two pan-sized trout (for two people). Salt and pepper the trout inside and out and saute in 2 Tb coconut oil. Remove the trout from the pan and add:

    1 Tb parboiled/ frozen basil, preferably lime basil, or 2 Tb fresh
        basil, chopped.
    1 Tb coconut oil
    1/4 cup chopped pistachios
    1 Tb lime juice + 2 tsp lime zest
    1 tsp honey
    1/4 tsp black pepper
    1/4 tsp salt

Off heat and cook gently 1 minute, scraping the pan. Meanwhile, debone the trout. Or you could use filets in the first place.

Roasted Red Pepper Coconut Sauce for Salmon

Charbroil 4 red bell peppers (or Sweet Italia) until the skin is black, then peel. It works best to peel under cold running water.

    2 shallots or scallions, chopped
    4 cloves chopped garlic (or use 2 tsp roasted garlic puree)
    1 Tb coconut oil

Saute the chopped shallots and garlic in the coconut oil. Reserve.

Puree the peppers and garlic with

> 1 Tb chopped fresh basil
> 1/2 cup dry white wine
> 1/2 tsp salt
> 2 Tb maple syrup

Place in a pan with the shallots and garlic and simmer 10-15 min., stirring frequently, then add

> 1/2 cup thick coconut milk and reduce to thicken. Serve with grilled salmon filets or steaks (or trout or other fish). Serves four.

Scallops, Smoked Trout, and Chanterelle Sauce for Pasta

> 3 Tb coconut oil
> 1/2 cup chopped celery
> 2 cloves garlic, chopped
> 1 Tb shallots or scallions, chopped
> 1 lb scallops (I like the small bay scallops)
> 1 pan-sized smoked trout*, broken into boneless pieces
> 1/2 lb fresh chanterelles, sliced (or an equivalent amount dried, say 1 cup)
> 1 cup dry white wine
> 2 cups fish stock*
> 2 Tb chopped fresh Italian parsley
> 1 Tb chopped fresh tarragon
> 1/4 tsp saffron, soaked (save soaking water)
> 1/2 tsp pepper
> 1 tsp salt
> 1 can thick coconut milk
> 2 tsp arrowroot powder

Saute celery, garlic and shallots for 2 minutes in coconut oil; Add sliced fresh or reconstituted dried chantereles (or morels or sweet tooths (hedgehog mushroom)). Saute until they begin to brown;

Add 1 lb scallops and saute until firm. Add pieces of boneless smoked trout, toss to coat then add wine, stock, herbs, salt. Cook for 5 minutes. Add coconut milk and bring to simmer. Thicken with 2 tsp arrowroot powder dissolved in 1 Tb water. Pour over shell pasta.

Orange Wine Sauce (for fish filets or scallops)

To serve two.

1 Tb shallots, chopped and sauteed in 1 Tb coconut oil;

Add

1 cup fresh orange juice
1 tsp grated orange zest
1 Tb fresh lime juice
1/2 tsp salt
1/4 tsp fresh ground white pepper
1/2 cup dry white wine
5 drops orange oil

Reduce down to about 1/2 cup. Then add 1/2 cup thick coconut milk (canned) and bring to a simmer.

Serves 2-4. Excellent with scallops

Shrimp and Mushroom Crepes

Make a batch of gluten-free crepes*

---

1 lb shrimp, peeled and deveined, and coarsely chopped
1/2 cup shallots, chopped
1/2 lb fresh chanterelles or morels or sweet tooths, coarsely chopped (or use 1 cup dried, soaked mushrooms)
4 Tb coconut oil
2 cups Shrimp Sauce*
1 tsp arrowroot dissolved in 1 Tb water

Sauté the shallots briefly in 2 Tb coconut oil, then add the fresh mushrooms and sauté until they begin to brown. Remove from the pan and set aside.

Add the remaining 2 Tb coconut oil and heat on high. Add the shrimp and sauté to sear the surface, until they become opaque. Return the mushrooms and shallots to the pan.

Add 1 ½ cups Shrimp Sauce. If needed, add the arrowroot and cook to thicken. It should be quite thick.

Place 2-3 Tb of the shrimp- mushroom mixture on each crepe. Roll up and place in a shallow oiled casserole. Top the crepes with the remaining 1/2 cup Shrimp Sauce.

Bake 20 minutes at 350 degrees.

Serves four.

Sauteed Trout with Tangerine-Almond Coating

For 2 servings of trout filets

   1/4 cup almond meal
   1/4 cup finely minced dried, reconstituted tangerine peel (or use
      grated fresh peel)
   1/2 tsp salt
   1/2 tsp black pepper
   1/2 tsp chipotle powder
   1/2 tsp turmeric powder
   2 Tb blue corn meal
   3 Tb coconut oil
   1 Tb avocado oil

Coat filets thickly and saute in the oils. Cook about 10 minutes per inch of thickness.

Other types of fish could be substituted.

Shrimp, Apricot, and Shallot Crepes with Cashew-Coconut Cream Sauce

Make a batch of gluten- free crepes.

-----

   1 lb shrimp, peeled, deveined, and coarsely chopped
   1/2 cup dried apricots, soaked and coarsely chopped
   1/2 cup shallots, chopped
   2 Tb coconut oil

2 cups Cashew-Coconut Cream Sauce*
1 tsp arrowroot dissolved in 1 Tb water (to thicken if needed)

Sauté the shallot in the coconut oil on high heat briefly. Then add the shrimp and sauté until opaque. Add the apricots and 1 ½ cups Cashew-Coconut Cream Sauce. Bring to a simmer and add arrowroot if needed to make it quite thick.

Place 2-3 Tb of filling on each crepe, roll up and place in a shallow oiled casserole. Top with the remaining 1/2 cup Cashew-Coconut Cream Sauce. Bake at 350 degrees for 20 minutes. Serves 3-4.

Smoked Trout, Whitefish, or Salmon

For several fish. If large, filet them or at least make a cut along the spine.

Brine

1 Gallon water
2 cups non-iodized pickling salt
2 cups xylitol, coconut sugar or organic cane sugar
1 Tb molasses
1/2 cup black soy sauce or tamari
1 tsp onion powder
1 tsp garlic powder (granulated garlic)
1 tsp black pepper
1 Tb chipotle pepper powder
1 Tb smoked paprika
1 tsp ground celery seed
1/2 tsp dry thyme

Brine (marinate) overnight in the refrigerator or somewhere cool.

I use a large commercial cambro container with a lid for this. Doing your smoking when conditions are cool makes it easier to access cool storage conditions for larger batches. I load up my cambro with frozen fish and let them thaw in the brine overnight.

Remove the fish from the brine, give them a quick rinse in cool water and let them air dry for an hour before cranking up the heat, to let the „pellicle" form which is said to be important.

Many people like to use a Little Chief electric smoker. I use my Oklahoma Joe pit barbeque with alder wood and try to keep the temperature between 150 and 200 degrees. Smoking may take 6 to 12 hours depending on the thickness of the fish. This is *hot smoking*, and the fish will not keep under refrigeration as long as *cold smoked* fish would. Cold smoke requires a different set up.

Smoked Salmon - Tarragon Coconut Topping for Fish Filets

1 cup coconut oil
1/2 cup boneless smoked salmon, trout or whitefish
1 Tb lemon juice
1 tsp sugar
1/4 tsp salt, or to taste
1/2 tsp white pepper
2 Tb chopped fresh tarragon
2 Tb chopped toasted almonds

Chop finely in a food processor and place 1 Tb portions on trout shortly before finished cooking, whether baked or broiled. Freeze in individual packets for quick convenient use.

Smoked Trout and Mushrooms in Coconut Cream Sauce

Saute in 1 Tb coconut oil

2 Tb minced shallots or scallions

2 minced garlic cloves

1+ cup diced or sliced fresh mushrooms (meadow mushrooms, oyster mushrooms, chanterelles or shrimp russula would be good, or use domestic crimini). 1/2 cup dried wild mushrooms can be substituted; Save the soaking water and substitute for stock.

When lightly browned, add

1/4 cup Madeira wine

1 ½ cup fish stock

1 can thick coconut milk

1/2 cup raw cashew butter

2 Tb minced fresh tarragon

Bring to a boil, reduce heat and simmer 5 minutes.

Add

1 smoked trout (10-12 inches long), skinned and carefully deboned and broken into small pieces. (Or substitute smoked salmon.)

Simmer 3 minutes.

Serve over pasta or rice, or thicken with arrowroot or coconut roux* and use as a filling for crepes.

Spiced Baked Oysters with Bacon and Spinach

8 slices bacon, sliced 1/4" crossways.

Cook in a skillet until it is beginning to brown, but not too much. Drain on a paper towel and reserve. Save the bacon fat.

3 dozen small oysters, removed from their juices, juices reserved.
1 pound fresh spinach

Place the spinach in a big pot of boiling salted water and cook uncovered for 5 minutes. Drain, return to the pot and cool under cold running water until thoroughly cold. Drain again and with your hand, press all the water out of the spinach. Coarsely chop the spinach and reserve.

The Sauce:

4 Tb coconut oil
4 cloves crushed, peeled finely minced garlic

2 shallots, finely chopped
2 tsp roasted, freshly ground Szechuan pepper
1/2 tsp salt
1/2 tsp freshly ground black pepper
1/2 tsp cayenne pepper
2 Tb soy sauce, tamari, or coconut aminos
2 tsp raw cashew butter
2/3 cup fish stock*
The reserved oyster juice

Sauté the garlic and shallot in the oil briefly, then add the other ingredients, stir to mix thoroughly, simmer 5 minutes to reduce, then reserve.

1 cup quinoa, cooked in 2 cups beef stock
2 Tb coconut oil, melted with the reserved bacon fat
12 large scallop shells, on 2 baking pans

In the bottom of each shell, place about 3 Tb cooked quinoa, spread out.

Top with the spinach, equally divided.

Place 3 oysters on top of the spinach, in each shell.

Top with the coconut oil and bacon fat, then the bacon slices.

Bake at 425 degrees for 15 minutes. Avoid over cooking the oysters. Top with the reserved sauce and serve immediately. Serves six.

Sweet and Sour Sauce for Fish

Saute

1 Tb. chopped shallot or scallion in
2 Tb coconut oil

Combine with:

> 2 Tb fresh orange juice
> 2 tsp orange rind zest
> 1/2 cup coconut sugar (or 1/2 cup xylitol)
> 1/2 cup water
> 1/2 cup raspberry vinegar
> 1 Tb fresh tarragon, chopped
> 2 tsp Dijon mustard
> 1 Tb basalmic vinegar
> 1 tsp poppy seeds
> 1/2 tsp salt

Simmer about 15 minutes to reduce, add 1/2 tsp cornstarch or arrowroot dissolved in a bit of water to thicken as needed. Pour over sautéed fish filets or add to broiled or baked fish halfway through their cooking. Serves 4 to 6.

Trout Baked with Roasted Tomato-Papaya Sauce

Two trout filets

Combine

> 1/4 cup roasted tomatoes*, chopped
> 1 tsp roasted garlic puree*
> 2 Tb soaked chopped dried organic papaya
> 1 Tb chopped basil, preferably lime basil
> 1 Tb gluten-free tamari sauce, soy sauce or coconut aminos
> 1/2 tsp salt
> 1/2 tsp freshly ground black pepper
> 2 tsp coconut oil

Coat the bottom of a shallow baking pan with the coconut oil and place the trout filets on it and top with the sauce. Bake at 450 degrees for 10 minutes. The general rule is 10 minutes per inch of thickness. This would work for other kinds of fish as well.

Serves two.

Trout Filets in Crepes with Mushroom Coconut Cream Sauce

Make a batch of crepes. You will need eight good sized crepes.

Make 2 cups Coconut Cashew Cream Sauce*. Set aside.

Sauté four filets, each cut into two 1 ½"-2" strips. Quickly sear the filet strips to seal the surface in

> 2 Tb coconut oil. Set aside.
> 1/2 lb fresh mushrooms, sliced (use morels or chanterelles, sweet tooths, oyster mushrooms, shrimp russula, candy caps, or domestic crimini mushrooms).
> 1/4 cup chopped shallots
> 2 Tb coconut oil

Sauté the shallots and mushrooms in the coconut oil until browned. Add 1 ½ cups Coconut Cashew Cream Sauce (reserve 1/2 cup) and bring to a simmer. Cook for 3 minutes. Set aside.

Oil a baking dish with coconut oil. Place a trout filet on each of 8 crepes. Top with the mushroom cream sauce (divided in 8 portions). Roll each crepe into a cylinder and arrange in the baking pan. Top with the reserved cream sauce. You may want to thin it a bit with thin coconut milk if it is too thick. Bake 25 minutes at 375 degrees. Serves four.

Poultry

Oyster Mushroom Braised Chicken

One 3 to 4 lb chicken
1 ½ lb fresh oyster mushrooms
1 large or 2 medium onions
1 Tb minced fresh ginger
1/4 cup avocado oil

Slice the oyster mushrooms into bite-sized pieces.

Cut the chicken into serving pieces, then into 2-3" pieces with kitchen shears, cutting through the bones.

Chop the onions into 1/2" pieces.

Saute the ginger, onions and mushrooms in 1/4 cup coconut oil + 2 Tb avocado oil until brown. Remove, leaving the oil.

Add 1/4 cup avocado oil to the pan and brown the chicken pieces. You might have to do it in two batches. Remove excess oil and the chunks of breast meat. Return the mushrooms and onions to the pan.

Add:

1 cups chicken stock*
2 Tb gluten-free tamari, soy sauce, or coconut aminos
1/2 cup dry white wine
1/2 tsp salt
1/2 tsp freshly ground black pepper
1 tsp crumbled tangerine peel, soaked in a bit of water.

Bring to a boil and simmer the legs and thighs for 25 minutes, partially covered. Skim fat and scum from the surface as it cooks. Return the browned chicken breast pieces and bring to a simmer and continue cooking for 15-20 minutes until done. Cooking the breast meat for a shorter period is a nice touch that ensures it is not overdone and dry. Or you could just use legs and thighs.

Thicken with 1 Tb arrowroot dissolved in 1 Tb water.

Oyster mushrooms grow in clumps on cottonwood logs and stumps in Montana's river bottoms in the spring and fall, and are common elsewhere. They are cultivated and can be purchased fresh in supermarkets.

Chicken Breast with Candy Cap Mushrooms in Coconut Cream Sauce

2 boneless chicken breasts
2 Tb coconut oil
1/2 cup dried candy cap mushrooms, reconstituted and drained (save soaking water)
1/4 cup shallots or scallions, chopped
1/4 cup Madeira wine
1/3 cup canned coconut milk
1/4 cup raw cashew butter
1/2 cup mushroom soaking water
1/2 tsp salt
1/2 tsp freshly ground white pepper

Saute the chicken breasts in coconut oil until brown. Remove and reserve.

Add shallots or scallions and mushrooms and sauté in the remaining coconut oil (add more if needed) until lightly brown.

Add Madeira, mushroom soaking water, coconut milk, salt and pepper. Return chicken breasts to the pan and simmer 15-20 minutes until just done.

Chicken Breasts in Orange Marmalade/Mustard Sauce

2 boneless chicken breasts (supremes)
2 Tb shallots or scallions, chopped
2 Tb coconut oil
1 Tb avocado oil
1/4 cup orange marmalade
1 Tb Dijon style mustard
1/2 cup dry white wine
1 cup brown chicken stock (or good beef stock)
Salt, pepper to taste
6-8 drops orange oil (optional)
1/2 cup thick coconut milk (canned)

Salt, then saute chicken breasts in coconut oil and avocado oil until brown. Remove chicken and saute chopped shallots or scallions in the remaining oil (add more coconut oil if needed). Then add the browned chicken breasts to the orange marmalade, mustard, white wine, chicken stock, optional orange oil and coconut milk. Simmer 12-15 minutes partially covered, remove the breasts and keep warm; simmer the sauce for 10 minutes to reduce. Thicken with 1 tsp arrowroot dissolved in 1 Tb water.

Chicken-Mushroom Crepes

Per dozen small (5") crepes or 8 large (7") crepes*.

Combine

2/3 cup gluten-free flour
1/2 tsp salt
3 eggs

1 ½-2 cups thin coconut milk (canned or boxed)
2 Tb coconut oil, melted
avocado oil

With a mixer, beat together until smooth. It should be thin enough to coat the pan with a thin layer. Let stand 1-2 hours.

Heat a 7-8" frying pan or crepe pan on medium high heat until hot. Coat the bottom with a thin layer of avocado oil. Using a 1/4 cup measure, pour 3 Tb or so of batter into the pan. Swirl the pan, coating the bottom with a thin layer. Cook for a minute or so until the bottom is nicely browned. Turn crepe over and cook briefly.

When cooked, place on a wax paper square on a plate. Cover with another square of wax paper.

As each crepe is cooked, add another square of wax paper to the pile. Add a little more avocado oil if it seems necessary. (The crepes can be frozen at this point for future use.)

———————————————

The mushroom- chicken filling (for 8 large crepes)

6 Tb coconut oil
1/2 lb fresh wild or domestic mushrooms such as crimini, sliced, or 1 cup dried wild mushrooms such as morels or chanterelles.
2 chopped shallots or scallions
1/2 lb diced chicken breast
1/4 cup gluten-free flour
1/2 tsp salt
1/2 tsp fresh ground white pepper
2 Tb Madeira wine
1 Tb cognac or brandy
1/2 cup mushroom soaking water, or chicken stock
1 cup Cashew-Coconut Cream Sauce* plus 1/2 cup for topping the crepes

Saute shallots in 3 Tb coconut oil with the fresh mushrooms until brown. If using dried, reconstituted mushrooms, squeeze out liquid and sauté lightly. When the mushrooms are sufficiently sautéed, add the Madeira wine and stir over heat so the mushrooms absorb the wine. Remove and set aside.

Toss the chicken breast meat with the gluten-free flour, salt and pepper. A one gallon baggie works well for this.

Add the remaining 3 Tb coconut oil to the pan and heat on high heat. Add the chicken breasts and brown them.

Return the mushrooms to the pan and add 2 cups coconut-cashew cream sauce* and the brandy, and mix. Have 3 cups of the sauce on hand, for the filling and topping.

Bring to the simmer and simmer, covered, for 10 minutes. Stir once or twice to prevent sticking.

Place 1/3 cup or so of the filling mix on top of a crepe, and roll it up. Repeat. Place the crepes in a baking dish oiled with coconut oil. Top with a dollop of coconut-cashew cream sauce on each crepe, spread out, and bake at 350 degrees for 25-30 minutes. Serve with a side of rice.

Chicken- Cashew- Pineapple Filling for Crepes

Make a batch of crepes*.

Sauté until browned in 2 Tb coconut oil

   2 boneless chicken breasts, sliced
   3 scallions, chopped

Remove the browned chicken breasts, and let cool. Dice 1/4".

Add to the pan:

The reserved chicken.

  1 cup chicken stock
  2 Tb Thai Hot Sweet Chili Garlic Sauce*
  1 cup pineapple, chopped
  1 cup toasted, salted cashews, chopped
  1/2 cup bell pepper, diced
  1/2 tsp freshly ground black pepper
  Salt to taste

Place about 1/3 cup of filling on each crepe, roll up and place in a baking dish which has been oiled with coconut oil. Top with this, well mixed:

  1 cup thick coconut milk
  1/2 cup raw cashew butter

Bake for 25-30 minutes at 350 degrees. Serves four.

Chicken Wings with Tangerine Sauce

Marinate 2 lb chicken wings for 15-30 minutes in

  2 Tb cornstarch
  2 Tb soy sauce
  1 Tb dry sherry

Brown in 1/4 cup avocado oil:

  4-5 pieces dried tangerine peel
  1+ tsp Thai or bird's eye hot peppers
  1 tsp Szechuan peppercorns, ground

Remove from the hot oil and set aside; then add the chicken wings to the hot oil, and brown.

At the conclusion, return the tangerine peel and hot peppers and add 1 chopped scallion and toss briefly, then add

 1 cup chicken bone broth or stock*
 1 Tb gluten-free soy sauce or tamari
 1 Tb coconut sugar or xylitol
 1 tsp roasted garlic

Cover and simmer 30- 40 minutes, stirring occasionally.

Chicken Breasts with Mangoes and Peppers

 4 skinless, boneless chicken breasts cut in 3/4" – 1" pieces.

Marinate in

 1 Tb arrowroot or organic, non-GMO corn starch for 15-30 minutes
 1 Tb gluten-free tamari sauce, soy sauce, or coconut aminos
 1/2 tsp salt
 1/2 tsp black pepper

Brown quickly in 2 Tb coconut oil; remove chicken and set aside.

Add another 2 Tb coconut oil to the pan and add

1 large onion cut in 1/2" pieces
1 cup serrano peppers, 1/4" dice (or other fresh hot pepper)
1 cup bell peppers, 1/2" dice
1 Tb minced ginger

Brown, then add

1/2 cup oven-roasted tomatoes* or 1 cup tomato puree
1 tsp roasted garlic puree*
1 cup dried, soaked mangoes, 1/2" dice plus the soaking water
1 tsp whole cumin seeds roasted, then freshly ground*
2 tsp freshly ground coriander seeds
1 tsp tumeric powder
1 tsp ancho chili powder
1 tsp garam masala spice mix
1/4 cup chopped basil
1/4 cup soaked golden raisins, drained
The reserved browned chicken
1 cup water

Simmer 10 minutes. Serves four.

Rosemary Honey Chicken

One 3 lb chicken, cut into pieces. Season with salt and pepper. Brown in

3 Tb coconut oil plus
2 Tb avocado oil.

Remove chicken and reserve in a casserole.

Saute in the remaining oil:

1 clove garlic, sliced
1 chopped shallot

Add 1/3 cup honey

> 4 sprigs fresh rosemary leaves, de-stemmed, bruised in a mortar, then chopped finely.
> 2 cups chicken stock
> 1/2 tsp salt
> 1/2 tsp black pepper
> 2" dried, soaked orange peel, chopped or 1 Tb fresh zest
> 1" dried, soaked lemon peel, chopped or 1 tsp fresh zest

Simmer sauce for 1/2 hour; strain. Pour over the browned chicken, and bake at 350 degrees for about 45 minutes, uncovered (cover loosely with parchment). Baste 2-3 times. Serve the chicken with the pan juices. Rice is good with this. Serves six.

Roasted Red Bell Pepper and Pecan Sauce

> 1 Tb coconut oil
> 2 shallots or scallions, chopped
> 1/4 cup char-roasted (blackened) red bell pepper, peeled and finely chopped
> 1/4 cup pecans, finely chopped
> 1/4 cup thick coconut milk
> 1 Tb Italian parsley, chopped
> 1/4 tsp black pepper
> 1/4 tsp salt

Sauté shallots or scallions in the coconut oil for 2 minutes. Add the rest of the ingredients and simmer for 2 minutes.

Serve with sautéed chicken breast. (Or with pork chops.) Serves two.

Sauté

    1 chopped shallot
    1 chopped garlic clove
    2 tsp chopped fresh ginger

in

    1 Tb coconut oil until just light brown, then add
    1 cup chicken stock or bone broth
    1/2 cup dry white wine and reduce by half,

then add

    1/2 cup fresh squeezed orange juice
    Zest of 1/2 orange
    1/4 cup roasted cashew butter
    1/4 cup mango chutney
    2 Tb orange marmalade
    2 tsp candied ginger
    1/2 tsp salt
    1/4 cup thick coconut milk
    1 tsp cayenne
    1/2 tsp ground star anise seeds
    1/4 tsp ground cardamom
    1/2 tsp freshly ground black pepper

Simmer for 10 minutes, stirring. Serve with sautéed chicken breasts (or pork chops).

Roasted Cornish Game Hens in Coconut-Rosemary Sauce

Two Cornish Game Hens. Salt inside & out and brush with olive oil. Roast 10 minutes at 450 degrees,

40 minutes at 350 degrees. Rest 5 minutes.

Serve with this sauce:

> 1 shallot, minced and sauté in
> 1 Tb coconut oil
> 1 Tb olive oil

Add

> 1/2 cup chicken bone broth or good stock*
> 2 Tb fresh rosemary leaves, bruised and finely minced
> 1/2 tsp fresh ground black pepper
> 1/2 cup thick coconut milk

Simmer 10 minutes; Thicken with 1/2 tsp organic non-GMO cornstarch or arrow root, dissolved in 1 tsp water. Substitute game birds such as grouse or pheasant.

Broiled Wild Duck Breast with Hot Gingered Garlic Duck Sauce

Quantity for two wild ducks, multiply as needed. Serves four. Remove the breasts from the breastbone and marinate, if you wish, with the Duck Marinade (below) for several hours or overnight. Chop up the rest of the carcass and make a duck stock out of it. (See the master recipe.)

To make the sauce:

Saute for 2 minutes in 1 Tb coconut oil:

  1 tsp finely chopped ginger
  1 minced scallion

then add

  2 Tb Hot Sweet Garlic Chili Sauce*
  2 tsp minced candied ginger
  1 cup concentrated duck stock
  1 Tb dried currants soaked in Madeira wine

Simmer for 2 minutes, thicken with 1 tsp arrowroot dissolved in water. Reserve.

Melt 1 Tb coconut oil in a small roasting pan, and coat the duck breasts with it, and season with salt and freshly ground black pepper.

Broil in an oven with top and bottom heat at 450 degrees for about 4-5 minutes on a side. They should be rare to medium rare. If they are over cooked they won't be as good.

Top with the chili sauce to serve.

Alternately, if you have breasts with the plucked skin in place, they could be grilled over charcoal.

Duck Marinade

  1 scallion, chopped
  1 tsp roasted garlic puree*
  1 Tb soy sauce or tamari or coconut aminos
  1 tsp raspberry vinegar

2 Tb white wine
1/2 tsp salt
1/4 tsp black pepper
1 tsp avocado oil

Marinate two boneless mallard (or other wild duck) breasts (supremes) overnight in the fridge.

Hanging (Aging) Poultry and Wild Game Birds

It is an old British and European tradition to hang game birds with the innards still in, for at least several days. I have long hung game birds, particularly ducks and grouse. Pheasants are said to respond well to hanging. The process renders them tenderer and more flavorful, increasing their natural flavor. It makes them easier to pluck also. It becomes a matter of personal taste just how much flavor you want. I now generally hang game birds 4-6 days at temperatures in the 40's or low 50's if possible. Older birds can be profitably hung for as long as a week. I have hung game birds in the past at room temperature. I've hung mallards for five days at room temperature, and found that they had a stronger flavor than I really wanted, but one of the guests just raved about them, declaring them to be the "finest duck I've ever had". More recently, I have hung mallards for up to six days in the high 40's, and they were tender and succulent but not strong.

If a bird is badly gut shot you will not want to hang it as long..

I have also hung large (6 lb) chickens from the local Hutterite colony for as long as six days at cool room temperature, and it makes them tender and succulent, with more chicken flavor. I will continue to experiment with timing and temperature.

Duck with Marinade and BBQ Sauce

Marinate one domestic duck overnight in the marinade.

Steam 2 ½ hours, then baste with remaining marinade.

Using an indirect heat smoke cooker, smoke cook 3-4 hours at about 250 degrees, spraying with dilute soy/sherry every 30-45 minutes, or use the gluten-free beer mop. Serve with the BBQ sauce.

Alternately, marinate boneless wild duck breasts overnight, and grill over charcoal for 4-5 minutes per side. Slather on the BBQ sauce prior to grilling. They should be rare to medium rare.

Duck Marinade

Per two boneless mallard breast halves: Combine

    1 scallion, chopped
    1 tsp roasted garlic puree
    1 Tb dark soy sauce or tamari sauce
    1 tsp raspberry vinegar
    1 Tb port wine
    1 Tb white wine
    1 Tb avocado oil

Double this for a whole duck. Marinate overnight in the fridge. (This marinade also works for venison steaks.)

BBQ sauce (enough for two mallard breast halves- quadruple for a whole domestic duck).

> Several drops orange oil
> 2 Tb soy sauce
> 1/4 cup Hoisin sauce
> 1 tsp Chinese 5 spice powder
> 1 Tb dry sherry
> 1/2 tsp salt
> 1 Tb avocado oil

Grouse Breast in Chanterelle Coconut Cream Sauce

Quantity to serve two. 1 small grouse breast per person, or half of a large one.

1/2 cup dried chanterelle mushrooms (or morels or sweet tooths or candy caps) per person, soaked in water, then strain and squeeze most of the liquid out. Save the soaking liquid. Or use 1 cup fresh sliced mushrooms per person.

Cut the meat from the breast bones and cut in 3/4" cubes. Toss with gluten-free flour mix and salt and pepper when ready to saute.

Make a grouse stock starting with chicken bone broth plus onions, carrots, garlic, parsley, thyme, bay leaf and browned grouse bones, legs, backs. I cut them up with kitchen shears. Strain and set aside.

2 shallots or scallions, chopped
1 garlic clove, chopped
1 Tb coconut oil
1 Tb avocado oil

Saute the shallot, garlic and drained chanterelles until they begin to brown. Remove and set aside.

Add more oil to the pan and saute the coated grouse meat until brown. Return the shallot, garlic, and chanterelles to the pan.

Add

1 cup grouse (or chicken) stock
1/2 cup dry white wine
The mushroom soaking liquid (if you used dry mushrooms)
1 cup thick (canned) coconut milk
1/4 cup raw cashew butter and simmer for 20 minutes. Taste for salt.
Serve over rice (or gluten – free pasta).

You could use this basic approach for chicken breasts or other game birds such as pheasants.

Grouse Breasts with Apple and Huckleberry

Marinate 4 blue grouse boneless breasts (supremes; two per bird), or 4 whole boneless ruffed grouse breasts, cut in half at the breastbone, at least 2-4 hours, or overnight in this marinade:

1/2 cup dry white wine
2 Tb Madeira wine
1 Tb gluten-free tamari or soy sauce, or coconut aminos

Drain and reserve the marinade.

Saute in 2 Tb coconut oil until beginning to brown:

> 1 minced peeled cooking apple
> 1 scallion or shallot, minced

Add

> 2 Tb huckleberry jam or syrup*
> 3 Tb Thai hot sweet garlic chili sauce*
> The reserved marinade
> 2 Tb Calvados or gluten-free unblended applejack (or Grand Marnier)
> 1/2 tsp salt

Simmer for 5-10 minutes until thickened and the apple is tender.

Grill the breasts over charcoal 4-5 minutes per side, or until just past the pink stage. You could also bake 15-20 minutes at 375 degrees. Blue grouse may take a little longer than ruffed grouse. Top with the warm sauce. Serves four. This recipe would also work for pheasant or chicken breasts.

Wok Omelet

> 4 eggs
> 1 Tb coconut oil
> 2 medium mushrooms, sliced
> 2 scallions, chopped or 4 garlic scapes, chopped
> 1 cup cooked rice
> 1 Tb Roasted Tomato Topping*, or use salsa*.
> Salt and pepper to taste.

Heat the oil in the wok, then add the scallions or scapes and mushrooms, saute 2-3 minutes. Move to the side of the wok. Add the rice (about 1/4" thick layer). Distribute the scallions or scapes and mushrooms on top of the rice. Break the eggs on top and add salt and pepper. Cover and cook on medium low until the eggs are substantially cooked, so that the omelet can be turned in one piece. Add the omelet topping and turn off the heat, cover, and let it finish cooking. Serves one or two.

Roasted Tomato Topping for Eggs

2 Tb coconut oil
1 cup roasted tomato, chopped
2 small onions or one large, finely chopped
1-4 cloves of garlic, finely chopped
1 Tb raisins
2 Tb chopped basil
1/2 tsp salt
1/2 tsp freshly ground black pepper

Saute onions and garlic in coconut oil until light brown, add the raisins, cook briefly, add the roasted tomatoes and basil and bring to a simmer, cook for 5 min.

Top omelets with this sauce.

Pork

Braised Sweet Pork

2 lbs pork, 1-1½" cubes

Saute until brown in 1/4 cup avocado oil
then add

1 Tb chopped garlic
2 scallions, chopped
and sauté 1 minute more

add

1/4 cup gluten-free dark soy sauce, tamari or coconut aminos
1/2 cup rice vinegar
3/4 cup xylitol or coconut sugar
1 Tb molasses
1 cup water or chicken stock
1 tsp star anise seed powder
3-4" dried orange peel, chopped finely
1/2 cup thick (canned) coconut milk

Simmer 40 minutes, then thicken with arrowroot and add 1 tsp toasted sesame oil (optional) Serves six. It would be good over rice.

Brown Berry Sauce for Ham

Saute

1 shallot, chopped
1 clove garlic, chopped in
1 Tb coconut oil

Add

    1 cup good brown stock (beef or chicken)
    1/2 cup Madeira wine
    1 Tb fresh tarragon, chopped
    1/2 tsp fresh ground black pepper

Simmer 15 minutes then add

    1/4 cup boysenberry or huckleberry preserves or syrup
    2 Tb chopped, roasted almonds.
    Serve with sautéed ham steaks.

See also
Fig – Pistachio Sauce for Venison or Pork*

Hot Peanut Sauce for Grilled Pork Chops

For 1 ½ lb grilled pork chops (or baked ham or grilled chicken).

Marinade:

    2 Tb dark soy sauce, tamari, or coconut aminos
    1 Tb Madeira wine

Sauce:

Saute in 1 Tb coconut oil:

    2 Tb minced garlic
    2 tsp minced fresh ginger (2 slices)
    1 Tb dried, soaked, chopped orange peel (or fresh zest)

then add

1/4 cup chunky peanut butter

1 Tb Szechuan hot bean paste or chili paste

2 Tb coconut sugar or xylitol

1 Tb molasses

2 Tb rice vinegar (or cider vinegar)

2 Tb orange marmalade

Mix and simmer 5 minutes. Serve.

Quick Sauce for Pork Chops

Per serving. Combine and melt together:

1 Tb tamari or soy sauce or coconut aminos

1 Tb Hot Sweet Chili Garlic Sauce*

1 tsp prepared Dijon style mustard

1 Tb orange marmalade

1 Tb coconut oil

Mustard – Huckleberry Sauce for Pork Chops

Another quick and easy sauce; for four servings.

Combine

1/4 cup Dijon style mustard

1/4 cup huckleberry syrup or jelly (or boysenberry).

1 tsp freshly ground black pepper

1 Tb coconut oil

Warm, then serve with sauteed pork chops (or ham).

Grilling is nice, but the ultimate in home BBQ is the smoke- cooking home pit barbeque unit, such as the Oklahoma Joe's which I own. An advantage, besides the incredible taste, is no fats are falling directly onto coals, because the fire box is separate from the barrel with the grill for meat so *that* cancer risk is avoided.

In order to cook meat on a smoke- cooking home pit barbeque unit, pit masters often employ a dry rub as a marinade, overnight. Sometimes also a large syringe is used to inject a marinade directly into the meat. If you were to filter some of the mop given below through a dishcloth, it could be used for this purpose without plugging up the syringe. The mop is otherwise used to baste the meat as it smokes and cooks. Toward the end of cooking BBQ sauce is slathered on.

Basic Dry Rub

   1/4 cup coconut sugar
   1/4 cup salt
   1/4 cup granulated (dry) onion
   2 Tb granulated garlic
   2 Tb smoked paprika
   1 Tb ancho chili powder
   1 Tb chipotle powder, or to taste
   1 Tb black pepper, freshly ground
   1 Tb Szechuan peppercorns, toasted and ground
   1 Tb coriander seeds, freshly ground
   1 Tb cumin seeds, toasted and freshly ground

Basic Mop

Barbequing pork ribs, or a whole chicken, will take several hours, depending on the temperature you maintain (I try for 250-275F), but you are burning wood such as alder, apple or hickory, so you have to

keep an eye on it and do the best you can. Basting with the „mop"
every 30-45 minutes is important to keep the meat from drying out.

Combine in a sauce pan:

> 12 ounces gluten-free beer
> 1/2 cup cider vinegar
> 1/4 cup balsamic vinegar
> 1/4 cup avocado oil
> 1 medium onion, finely minced
> 2 garlic cloves, finely minced (or 1 tsp roasted garlic)
> 1 Tb of the basic rub, above

Simmer 25 minutes. Strain. This can also be injected into large cuts.

BBQ Sauce

Saute in

> 2 Tb coconut oil until the onions are translucent:
> 1 onion, chopped
> 1 Tb chopped garlic
> 1 Tb chopped ginger

Add

> 1 ½ cups orange juice
> Zest of 1 orange
> 12 drops concentrated orange oil
> 2 cups chopped pineapple
> 1 cup apricot preserves
> 1/4 cup dark rum
> 2 Tb ketchup (for ham) or 1 cup (pork ribs, chicken, beef)
> 2 Tb tomato paste* (for ham) or 1/2 cup (ribs, chicken, beef)
> 2 cups organic cider vinegar
> Juice of 1 lemon + zest
> Juice of 1 lime + zest

1/2 tsp ground allspice
1/2-1 tsp cayenne
1 tsp ancho chili powder
1/2 cup coconut sugar + 1 dropper stevia
1 tsp chipotle pepper powder
1/4 tsp fresh ground nutmeg
1/2 tsp star anise seeds, ground
1 tsp coriander, fresh ground
1 tsp paprika
1 tsp roasted, ground Szechuan pepper
1 tsp fresh ground black pepper
1/4 cup gluten free dark soy sauce, tamari, or coconut aminos
Salt to taste

Simmer for 30 minutes or so to thicken. Strain and puree the chunks and return to the pan to simmer for another 10 minutes. Optional: off heat, stir in 2 Tb horseradish. Serve.

Rosemary-Apricot BBQ Sauce

Sauté in

2 Tb coconut oil until beginning to brown:
1/2 cup chopped shallots or scallions
2 cloves chopped garlic

Add

1/2 cup fresh rosemary leaves, bruised in a mortar
1/4 cup gluten-free black soy sauce, tamari, or coconut aminos
1/2 cup dry white wine
1/4 cup cider vinegar
1/2 cup roasted tomatoes, pureed or chopped
1/2 cup water
1/4 cup brandy or cognac

Simmer slowly for 1/2 hour, then strain.

Add the strained rosemary sauce, and

> 1 cup apricot preserves
> 1/2 cup honey
> 2 Tb ketchup
> 1 Tb gluten-free Worcestershire sauce
> 1 Tb candied ginger, finely minced
> 1/2 tsp ground cardamom seeds
> 1/2 tsp Dave's Insanity Sauce or cayenne to taste
> 1 tsp black pepper
> 1/2 tsp salt, or to taste

Simmer 50 minutes, stirring, until reduced and thick.

Serve with barbequed pork ribs or grilled pork chops.

Sautjed Pork Loin Scallops with Apple Butter Sauce

Saute

> 1 Tb minced shallots in
> 1 Tb coconut oil

Add

> 1/4 cup demiglace sauce plus 1/2 cup water (or 1 cup good beef stock)
> 1/2 cup Madeira wine
> 1/3 cup apple butter
> 1/4 cup applejack or calvados
> 2 tsp apple cider vinegar

Simmer 10 min. Thicken with 1/2 tsp arrowroot dissolved in 1 Tb water. Serve with sautéed pork loin. Serves 4-6.

Sauce for Grilled Pork Chops (or fish or chicken)

Saute in

2 Tb coconut oil:
2 Tb chopped shallots

Add:

1/2 cup grape jelly or elderberry jelly
1/4 cup Madeira wine
2 Tb Balsamic vinegar
1/2 tsp salt
1 tsp roasted garlic puree*
1/3 cup water

Simmer 5 minutes to thicken.

Serves four. Optional additions:

2 roasted (blackened) and peeled red bell peppers or other sweet pepper, pureed.
2 Tb thick coconut milk (for fish or chicken breasts).

Rosemary, Honey and Garlic Sauce

To serve over sautéed pork chops, venison steaks, burger, or lamb chops.

This is the amount of sauce per serving. Sauté the meat and reserve.

Deglaze the pan with 2 scallions or shallots, chopped, in

> 1 Tb coconut oil

Sauté for a minute or two and then add, scraping:

> 1 tsp fresh or frozen rosemary leaves, chopped
> 1/2 tsp roasted garlic puree
> 1 Tb honey
> 1/4 tsp black pepper
> 1/4 tsp salt
> 2 Tb dry white wine
> 1 tsp gluten free soy sauce, tamari, or coconut aminos

Pour over the sautéed meat.

Can be served over rice, or for a more paleo approach, skip the rice.

Venison, Lamb, and Small Game

Venison on the Hoof and the Plate

Venison (for our purposes, deer, elk, caribou, moose, and –though not actually related-- pronghorn) is, properly prepared, the finest red meat in the world. I usually put venison on the table in preference to beef, lamb, or bison, thus the focus of this book in that regard. Venison has long had a reputation as the premier meat of Europe, reserved only for the tables of the aristocracy. In American cities, venison raised on game farms commands very high prices in restaurants and specialty markets. The pronghorn, often incorrectly called antelope, is not actually an antelope, as found in Africa and Eurasia. This animal is related to nothing else on the planet. It is found on the western plains.

So why is it, then that a great many hunters and their families and dinner guests regard venison, especially deer and pronghorn, as a barely edible meat suited, at best, for salami. There is a particular flavor, known as gaminess, that most (but not all) people find unpleasant. A very strong gamey taste can render an animal inedible for most people. Too many deer and pronghorn acquire a gaminess that they do not need to have, because hunters and butchers do certain things incorrectly. (I think this is true to a lesser extent of elk and moose, which are less susceptible to gaminess. For reasons that are probably related, these animals are not quite as tasty as deer or pronghorn. They are also coarser and tougher.)

Gaminess enters the meat when, during field dressing, the hunter allows hair, especially urine-soaked hair to get on and stay on the meat.

Or cuts the urethra so that urine sprays directly onto cut surfaces of the meat. The bucks, especially, have musk glands in the vicinity of their hind knees that soak the hair in the region with musk, and this can also contribute to gamey meat.

What to do? First, field dress and transport the animal with care, to avoid the above problems. (Skin pronghorns as soon as possible, to get rid of the hair and allow for quick cooling. Ideally, they should be skinned in the field and wrapped in clean cloth for transport.) The hunter should also cut off the musk glands from both bucks and does. The musk glands are on the inside of the hind knee under the skin.

It is sufficient to remove the skin from the vicinity, the glands will come off with the skin. Avoid slicing through the tendon on the rear of the knee; otherwise it will be difficult to hang. Then clean the blade before you cut anywhere near any meat. Try to keep it clean.

Clean the animal with a damp rag when you hang it, removing any stray hairs. People do things to game they would recoil in horror from if they thought their beef had been handled that way!

If at all possible, hang the animal, skinned and covered with a cheesecloth bag, in a cool, dry garage or shed secure from animals, or better yet, in a meat locker, for at least seven to 10 days, up to three weeks.

Hanging meat tenderizes it as autolytic enzymes begin to break down the fibers. If it gets a little moldy, generally this doesn't hurt anything. You just trim it off along with the outer filament. (I did encounter a mold once which was bad news. It grew on pronghorns hanging in a musty old basement, and proved to be highly invasive, penetrating deeply into the muscle, and really tasted terrible.) The L.L. Bean Game and Fish cookbook recommends not skinning them until you are ready to butcher, but if you let it freeze, then it will be really hard to skin.

Secondly, when the animal is butchered, if you take the short and easy route, you will end up with inferior, gamey, tough meat. Many people bone and cut the meat into random chunks with steaks cut right through muscle masses, and including chunks or sheets of fat, tendons (gristle), and filaments. Or they take it to a commercial butcher, where the quarters are sometimes cut with a bandsaw into steaks and roasts familiar to consumers, including all the fat and gristle and frequently bone. Bone and fat are repositories for the gamey flavor, and you must cut them away from the meat. This is a tedious and time-consuming process, but crucial if you want gourmet-quality meat. Venison fat also gets rancid in the freezer. And gristle, of course, makes the meat tough! Pit-barbequed venison ribs can be excellent, but you will necessarily be eating some fat, so don't try to keep them frozen very long. Venison fat is fine when it is hot, but when it gets cold, it is not palatable. Take one or two ribs from the heat to your plate at a time. A Sawzall reciprocating saw works great to cut ribs to serving size (4-5") and separate them from the backbone.

More complete BBQ instructions are on page 115.

The Sawsall also works well for cutting the head off and separating the hind quarters. Leg bones can be cut up for stock, in 3-4" pieces. To butcher venison properly, take a sharp flexible knife and strip off the outer layer of dried sheath and fat, then separate the individual muscle masses and remove them from the bone one at a time. To do this, tease an opening with your knife and fingers and follow the muscle mass around, separating it from the adjoining muscle. Each muscle will have an outer layer of filament. Strip off this filament and cut off any tendons, wasting as little meat as possible. Save scraps for stock, everything but the fat.

Remove and discard any small clumps of fat. Look carefully to find any filamentous sheaths that dive into the interior of the muscle. Carefully cut these out. Practice will make this easier, as will a very sharp knife. This process results in smaller steaks than you would get otherwise, but they are prime, prime, prime! Be sure to wrap well with freezer paper to avoid freezer burn, and label the packages (i.e., whitetail buck, loin, 2018). It helps to avoid freezer burn if you place wrapped steaks in large plastic Tupperware type containers. I put stew meat and boneless bits in a baggie, then wrap that with freezer paper. A small straw helps you get all the air out of the baggie.

So for steaks (and salami and stir-fry, for that matter), you have removed all the gristle material, and all the fat, and you end up with beautiful lean red meat.

I leave gristle in stew meat, because it is necessary to ensure a moist and succulent end result.

Traditional European venison cookery usually employed elaborate marinades to cover up the gaminess and to tenderize the meat. With this method of preparation, this is generally not necessary. However, it can happen, particularly if you shoot a big old buck in the rut. Their bodies are pumped full of hormones and adrenalin, their hair is soaked with musky urine, and they can be gamey despite your best efforts. On the theory that antlers are not edible, you might consider not shooting these bucks during the rut. Also, what the animals have been feeding on can have some effect on the quality of the taste. If there is a problem of this sort in your area, hunt elsewhere.

In your search for recipes, venison can be substituted for lamb in many dishes, particularly Indian curries, or can be substituted for beef in Chinese stir-fries. Or, if you don't have venison for recipes in this book, substitute bison, lamb or grass-fed beef. If the sauce would appear to work for that, you're all set.

Sautéed Venison Steaks

Sprinkle the steaks with salt just prior to cooking. I use high temperature avocado oil. Heat on high, and quickly sear both sides of the steaks. Reduce heat to medium low to finish. Cook to medium rare. Serve with any of the following sauces, or sauces listed in the Sauces chapter.

Apple Szechuan Pepper Venison Sauce

1 scallion or shallot, chopped
1 Tb coconut oil
1 cup concentrated beef or venison stock
2 Tb apple butter
1 tsp roasted ground Szechuan peppercorns
1/2 tsp roasted garlic puree
1/2 tsp salt
1/2 tsp freshly ground black pepper
If you wish, you could add one or both of these:
1 Tb preserved (pickled) grated horseradish (optional)
2 Tb chopped pistachios (optional)

Saute the scallion or shallot in the coconut oil for 1 minute, then add the beef stock, apple butter, garlic, Szechuan pepper, salt, and black pepper. Bring to a simmer and cook for 20 minutes to reduce to about 1/2 cup. Taste for seasonings and turn off the heat. Add the horseradish or pistachios if desired.

Serve with sauteed or grilled venison steaks. Two servings.

Candy Cap Mushroom Sauce for Venison

1/2 cup dried candy cap mushrooms, reconstituted and lightly squeezed (save water)
1 Tb shallot, chopped
2 Tb coconut oil
1/4 cup Madeira wine
1 Tb Demiglace sauce (or 1/4 cup venison stock or good beef stock)
1/2 cup dry white wine
1/2 cup mushroom soaking water

1/2 tsp salt
1/2 tsp freshly ground black pepper
1 tsp arrowroot powder dissolved in 1 Tb water

Saute shallot and mushrooms in coconut oil for 2-3 minutes.

Add Madeira, Demiglace sauce or stock, white wine, salt, pepper, and water. Reduce by half. Thicken with arrowroot (or organic, non-GMO cornstarch) and taste for salt. Experiment with other mushrooms if you like.

Serve. Enough for two servings of sautéed venison steaks. (Or you could substitute pork chops.)

Date-Madeira Sauce for Venison

Saute venison steaks (to serve 4) in

2 Tb avocado oil or coconut oil

Remove steaks, and to the pan juices, add and reduce while stirring and scraping:

2 shallots or scallions, chopped
1/2 cup Madeira wine
1 cup good beef (or venison) stock
1/4 cup fresh orange juice
1 tsp orange zest
4 chopped dates
1/4 tsp allspice
1 Tb chopped fresh tarragon
Salt and pepper to taste

For two servings. Combine:

> 2 Tb Hot Sweet Chili Garlic Sauce*
> 2 Tb prepared horseradish
> 1 Tb gluten-free soy sauce, tamari, or coconut aminos
> 1/2 tsp freshly ground black pepper
> 1/2 tsp salt

Mix and warm, and pour over sautéed or grilled salted venison steaks.

Combine:

> 1/4 cup roasted tomatoes*, chopped
> 1 Tb Hot Sweet Chili Garlic Sauce*
> 1 tsp roasted garlic puree*
> 2 tsp raspberry vinegar
> 1 tsp tawny port
> 1 tsp gluten-free soy sauce, tamari, or coconut aminos
> 1/2 tsp salt, 1/2 tsp freshly ground black pepper

Simmer 1 minute and serve.

Szechuan pepper rub

Combine

> 2 tsp roasted, ground Szechuan peppercorns*
> 1 tsp salt

1/2 tsp freshly ground black pepper
2 scallions or shallots, chopped
1 Tb avocado oil

Coat venison steaks heavily with the spice mixture. Heat the oil on medium high and sauté the scallion or shallot briefly, move to the side of the pan, and add the venison steaks. Sauté to medium rare. Serves two.

Spiced Szechuan Salt

Related to the above rub, you can make this, put it in a spice jar, and have it on hand. Coat venison steaks and sauté in coconut oil for a quick and easy meal.

1/4 cup roasted, ground Szechuan peppers
2 Tb salt

Fig – Pistachio Sauce for Venison or Pork

2 scallions or shallots, chopped and sauteed in 1 Tb coconut oil

Add

1/2 cup dried figs, chopped
1 Tb Hot Sweet Chili Garlic Sauce*
1 Tb Balsamic vinegar
1 tsp tamari or gluten free soy sauce, or coconut aminos
1/2 cup water
1/4 tsp salt

Simmer for 5 minutes

Add

1/4 cup pistachios, chopped

Thicken with 1/2 tsp arrowroot dissolved in 1 Tb water.

Serve with sauteed venison steaks or pork chops.

For 3-4 servings.

Spiced Brown Venison Sauce with Orange Marmalade

1 scallion or shallot, chopped
1 Tb coconut oil
1 cup brown beef stock or venison stock*
1 Tb orange marmalade
1/4 cup Madeira wine
1/2 tsp roasted garlic puree*
1 tsp candied ginger, minced
1/2 tsp salt
1/2 tsp Chinese 5 spices
1 Tb fresh chervil, chopped (or substitute 2 tsp chopped fresh
     tarragon)

Saute the chopped scallion or shallot in the coconut oil for 1 minute. Add the other ingredients and bring to a brisk simmer. Cook until the sauce is reduced to 1/2 cup.

Serve over sauteed or grilled venison steaks.

Makes two servings.

Wild Mushroom Brown Sauce

Use with morels, cepes, sweet tooths, chanterelles, meadow mushrooms, etc.

Soak 1/4 cup dried cepes (Boletus edulis; porcini) in 1/2 cup water.

Soak 1 cup dried mushrooms of your choice in 1 cup water (save the soaking water), or use 2 cups fresh wild mushrooms, sliced. Or you could use 1/2 cup Duxelles (page).

Saute 2 Tb chopped scallions or shallots in 2 Tb coconut oil briefly, saute fresh mushrooms until lightly browned, or toss the drained and squeezed soaked mushrooms (save the soaking water) briefly (2-3 minutes) in the hot oil. Reserve.

Combine

    1/2 cup dry white wine
    1 Tb cognac or French brandy
    2 Tb Madeira wine and reduce. Set aside and reserve.

To 2 cups homemade concentrated brown beef or venison stock or bone broth, or organic beef broth plus 1 Tb commercial gluten free beef stock base, add

    1 small carrot, sliced
    1/2 cup diced celery
    The mushroom soaking liquids, if any
    1 tsp tomato paste or 1 Tb roasted tomato puree*
    1/2 tsp fresh thyme or 1/4 tsp dried
    1/4 tsp ground marjoram or 1/2 tsp fresh
    2 Tb Italian parsley, chopped
    1 tsp fresh tarragon
    1 small bay leaf
    1 allspice berry

Simmer 30 min. Remove herb bag and strain. Return to the pan.

Return the reserved mushrooms to the pan and add

1/4 tsp freshly ground black pepper
Pinch crumbled saffron soaked in 1 Tb warm water (optional)

Simmer 30 minutes.

Thicken with arrowroot or non-GMO cornstarch if needed.

Salt to taste.

Serve over sauteed venison steaks (or lamb, pork or beef).

Venison Steaks with Hazelnut-Apple Sauce

Saute 2 minced shallots or scallions

1 minced garlic clove

in

2 Tb coconut oil

until lightly brown, then add and reduce for 2 minutes:

1/2 cup red wine

then add

1 peeled, minced apple
1 minced carrot
2 cups venison stock or beef stock
1/2 cup fresh apple juice

Tie in a cheesecloth bag:

> 1/2 tsp sage or 1 fresh leaf
> 1/4 tsp thyme or 1 small sprig
> 1 tsp grated orange rind
> 1 Tb chopped parsley

Simmer for 10 minutes, remove the herb bag, and thicken with 2 tsp arrowroot powder dissolved in 2 Tb water . Add 1/2 cup toasted, peeled and chopped hazelnuts. Makes 2+ cups, 4 generous servings. This is a thick, hearty sauce.

Sauteed Venison Steaks with Chipotle Onions and Garlic

Per serving: Heat a frying pan with

> 1 Tb avocado oil
> 2 Tb coconut oil

Add 1 small onion, sliced

> 1 clove garlic, chopped
> 1/2 + tsp chipotle pepper
> 1/2 tsp salt
> 1/2 tsp black pepper

Cook on medium high for 2-3 minutes. Move them to the side of the pan. Watch that they don't burn, stirring occasionally. Salt the venison steak and cook until medium rare, perhaps 4-5 min. per side. Top with the onion mixture.

Alternative flavoring: Hot Szechuan pepper and onions

> 1/2 cup sauteed sliced onion

Combined with

> 1/2 tsp cayenne pepper
> 1/2 tsp salt
> 1 tsp Szechuan peppercorns, roasted in a pan until they smoke, then ground in a mortar or spice grinder.

Venison Steaks Sautéed with Black Seed and Mustard Seed

Black seed (Nigella sativa or Kalonji) is one of those spices (like turmeric) that has a long list of health benefits, including being anti-cancer. It is used in Indian cuisine.

It is also known (inaccurately) as Roman coriander, black sesame, black cumin, black caraway and black onion seed.

> 2 servings of venison steaks
> 1/2 cup onions, thin sliced 1" pieces
> 1 tsp black seed
> 1 tsp black mustard seed
> 1/2 tsp salt
> 2 Tb coconut oil

Crush the seeds in a mortar, combine with salt, and coat the steaks heavily. Add about 1 tsp spice mixture to the onions.

Sauté the onions in the coconut oil until beginning to brown. Move to the side of the pan, press some of the oil out, and sauté the venison on medium high until medium rare. Stir the onions occasionally.

Top the steaks with the onions and serve.

Braised Venison With Currants, Apples, and Chinese Spices

1 lb venison scraps, free of gristle, about 1/2-3/4", or use cut-up steaks.
1 Tb fresh ginger, minced
1 large onion, cut in 1/2" pieces
2 medium apples, peeled and cut in 1/2" pieces
1 tsp roasted, ground Szechuan peppercorns
1/2 tsp cayenne pepper
1/2 tsp salt
1/4 cup black soy sauce or 1/3 cup tamari sauce
2 cups venison or beef bone broth or stock*
1/2 tsp ground star anise seeds
1 Tb dry sherry
1/4 cup dried currants
(1/4 cup dried apricots, optional. 1/2" pieces.)

Saute the fresh ginger in 3 Tb coconut oil plus 2 Tb avocado oil for about a minute, then add the onion and cook on high heat until the onion begins to brown, lower the heat to medium and finish browning. Remove onions and add the apples to the oil.

Brown the apples, and remove and set aside.

Add more avocado oil if needed and add the venison to the pan. Saute on high heat until brown, in two batches if necessary.

Then add the Szechuan peppercorns, cayenne pepper, and salt. (If browning in batches, add to the last batch.)

Return the onion to the pan and toss with the spices and venison. Cook for a minute or two, then add the black soy sauce or tamari sauce, stock, star anise, dry sherry, currants and optional apricots.

Simmer partially covered for one hour, then add the reserved apples and cook for another 30 minutes. If using stew meat with gristle, simmer 3 hours or until tender before you add the apples.

Thicken with 2 tsp arrowroot dissolved in 1 Tb water.

Good served over rice. Serves 4-5.

Ragout of Venison (or Lamb) with Figs

2 lb of venison (or lamb) stew meat cut in 3/4" to 1" cubes. Brown in 2 Tb coconut oil and 2 Tb avocado oil. Remove from pan, and add
2 coarsely chopped onions plus more oil as needed
2 tsp minced fresh ginger

Brown the onions and ginger. Combine meat, ginger and onions with:

1 cup figs, quartered
1 can coconut milk
4 cups venison (or beef) stock*
2 tsp roasted garlic
2 tsp Garam Masala spice mix

1/2 tsp ground cardamon seeds
1 tsp ground coriander seeds
1 tsp Chinese five spice powder
1 tsp salt
1/2 cup Madeira wine
2 tsp chopped fresh marjoram or oregano

If you have stew meat, which properly has a lot of gristle (tendons and filaments) so it will be tender and succulent with long simmering, cook on a simmer partially (mostly) covered for 3 hours.

If you have meat with little or no gristle, cook for only 1 hour.

Thicken with gluten and dairy-free roux. To make it, cook 1 Tb coconut oil and 1 Tb avocado oil with 2 Tb gluten free flour mix. (I used Namaste gluten free organic „Perfect Flour Blend" from Costco.) Cook on low heat for 5-10 minutes until it is nicely brown, stirring nearly constantly. Whisk it into the Ragout and simmer for 5 minutes to thicken.

Hot Chocolate Sweet Chili Garlic Sauce for Venison

2/3 cup Thai Hot Sweet Chili Garlic Sauce*
1/4 cup good unsweetened dark chocolate or raw cacao powder
1 Tb coconut oil

Mix together and heat gently to dissolve the chocolate. Serve with sauteed vension steaks.

Serves four. Thx to Ilo for the idea

Ragout of Venison with Wild Mushrooms

1 ½ lb venison stew meat in 3/4" - 1" cubes. Coat with gluten-free flour, salt, and pepper.

Saute 2 medium chopped onions (1/2" pieces) in 1/4 cup coconut oil until brown. Remove to a large heavy bottomed kettle.

Add 1/4 cup avocado oil and add the venison to the pan and saute on high heat until brown, scraping and stirring to prevent burning. Add more oil as needed.

Add to the pan and deglaze, scraping

> 1/4 cup red wine
> 2 cups concentrated venison or beef stock*

Remove to the kettle.

Soak 1 cup dried mushrooms such as sweet tooths or oyster mushrooms. This dish was excellent with Spring agrocybe mushrooms, which grow in my yard. If you have 1/2+ lb fresh wild mushrooms, saute them until brown in 1/4 cup coconut oil or rendered organic fat. Alternately, you could use 1 cup Duxelles*.

Also soak 1/4 cup dried cepe (porcini) mushrooms.

Add the mushrooms to the kettle with the onions and venison and add:

> 1/2 cup red wine
> 1 Tb roasted garlic*

3 cups of water (or stock if you did not use concentrated stock, above)

Simmer partially covered for 3-4 hours until the venison is tender. Stir to keep from sticking and burning. Add more water as needed.

Add salt and pepper to taste. If you prefer, you could bake it at 325 degrees in a covered casserole for 3 hours

Stir-Fried Venison with Beets, Onions, and Carrots

1 lb venison steaks, sliced in thin pieces 1"x 1/2".
1 Tb arrowroot or cornstarch
1 Tb gluten-free soy sauce, tamari, or coconut aminos
1 Tb dry sherry

Combine and marinate the venison for 1-4 hours, then stir-fry in

1 Tb coconut oil
1 Tb avocado oil
1 tsp salt

A wok works best; cook in two batches on high heat until the surface is sealed. Remove the venison and reserve. To the wok add

1 Tb coconut oil; heat and add
1 Tb fresh ginger, minced. Cook briefly, then

add

1 large onion, quartered and sliced
2 garlic cloves, minced

Stir-fry the ginger, onion, and garlic until the onions are translucent.

Add

1 ½ cups roasted, shredded beets
1 cup shredded carrots
2 Tb dried currants, soaked and drained

Stir-fry for 3 minutes, then add

> 1 cup venison or beef stock or bone broth*.
> 1 Tb gluten-free soy sauce, or tamari
> 1 Tb dry sherry
> 1 tsp coconut sugar
> 1 tsp ground star anise seeds

Bring to the simmer and cook, covered, for 5 minutes. Serves four, on a bed of rice.

Stir-Fried Venison with Peppers, Cashews, and Mangoes

1 lb boneless, fat and gristle- free venison cut about 1" by 1/2" by 1/4". Or so. This is to use up scraps, or you could cut up steaks.

Marinate for 15-30 minutes in

> 2 Tb gluten-free black soy sauce, tamari, or coconut aminos
> 1 Tb dry sherry

Then mix and coat with

> 1 Tb arrowroot or cornstarch

Stir-fry over high heat with

> 1/4 cup avocado oil
> 1 tsp salt

in two batches, until the surfaces are seared. Remove and set aside.

Add

 2 Tb coconut oil to the pan, add
 1 Tb minced ginger, stir-fry briefly, then add
 1 cup raw cashews (chopped into large pieces).

Stir-fry for a couple of minutes, then add

 1 ½ cups julienned carrots
 1 cup julienned bell or sweet italia peppers
 1/2 cup diced serrano or jalapeno peppers
 2 scallions, chopped

Stir-fry for 5-6 minutes until the carrots and peppers are mostly cooked. Add

 3/4 cup sliced (1/4") soaked dried mangoes

Stir-fry for a minute, then add

 1 Tb black soy sauce
 1 tsp dry sherry
 1 Tb gluten-free Hoisin sauce (available commerically)
 1 cup mango soaking water

The partially cooked venison

Bring to a simmer, cover, and cook on medium low for 3-4 minutes.

Serve over rice. Serves 3-4.

Venison Stir-fried with Pak Choi and Mushrooms

This is a fairly standard Chinese stir-fry.

> 2/3 lb venison, cut about 1" x 1/4"
> 2 Tb arrowroot or cornstarch
> 1 tsp ginger, minced
> 1 scallion, sliced
> 3 Tb avocado oil
> 2 cups pak choi, sliced
> 1 cup carrots, julienned
> 1/2 cup dried shitake mushrooms, soaked in 1/2 cup water (save)
>   or use fresh shitake.
> 2 Tb gluten-free soy sauce, tamari, or coconut aminos
> 1 tsp dry sherry
> 1/2 tsp arrowroot or cornstarch dissolved in a bit of water

Coat venison with the arrowroot and brown in the oil. Remove and set aside.

Stir-fry ginger briefly in the remaining oil then add carrots, drained and squeezed mushrooms and scallions and cook for 4-5 minutes, scraping any residue from the venison. Then add pak choi and stir-fry 2-3 minutes.

Add the mushroom soaking water, soy sauce and sherry. Return the venison to the pan, bring to a boil and simmer covered for 3 minutes.

Thicken with arrowroot and serve over rice. Serves two.

Venison or Beef Burger in Curried Coconut Sauce

Sauté 2/3 pound burger (1" pieces) in coconut 2 Tb coconut oil until brown. Remove and reserve.

In the same pan, sauté

- 2 tsp minced ginger
- 1 cup chopped onion
- 2 cloves garlic, minced
- 1/2 cup bell pepper, chopped.
- 2 Tb green or red hot pepper. If the peppers are fresh, sauté them. If they were par-cooked and frozen, add them after the onions, garlic and ginger have been sautéed until beginning to brown.

Add

- 2 Tb roasted tomatoes, chopped
- 2 Tb fresh basil, chopped
- 2 Tb fresh cilantro, chopped
- 1 tsp garam masala spice mix
- 1/2 tsp turmeric
- 1 tsp freshly toasted cumin seeds, ground
- 1 tsp coriander seed, freshly ground
- 1/2 tsp black pepper, ground. Grind the cumin, coriander and pepper together.
- 1 cup cultured coconut yoghurt

(Optional- 1/2 tsp cayenne pepper, or to taste.)

Simmer together for 2 minutes. Combine with the sautéed burger and bake for 25 minutes at 350 degrees. Serves two.

Roasted Red Pepper - Hazelnut Sauce

Serve with venison or lamb steaks or burger. Beef can be substituted.

   2 Tb coconut oil
   2 shallots or scallions, chopped
   1/4 cup char-roasted bell pepper (blackened), peeled and finely
       chopped or pureed
   1/4 cup freshly roasted, peeled hazelnuts, finely minced
   1/4 cup thick coconut milk
   1/2 tsp roasted garlic
   1/4 tsp freshly ground black pepper
   1/4 tsp salt

Sauté the shallots in the coconut oil for 2 minutes. Then add the pepper, hazelnuts, coconut milk, garlic, pepper and salt. Simmer 2 minutes.

Serves four.

Venison Burger with Sauces

Serve the following sauces with sautéed venison burger patties, or with venison steaks. Beef or lamb burger can be substituted.

Salt the burger(s) and sauté in coconut oil until medium rare. Remove from the pan and keep warm.

Deglaze the pan with one of these sauces, scraping, and reduce until thick. Top the burgers with the sauce and serve. I serve this dish over rice. **These amounts are for one serving.**

Sauté one chopped scallion in the oil remaining in the pan, and add:

1 tsp gluten-free Worcestershire sauce

1/4 cup dry red wine

1/2 tsp roasted garlic puree*

2 Tb bell pepper, chopped (if par-cooked and frozen, use as is. Otherwise, sauté first along with the scallions.)

1 Tb roasted tomato, chopped

1/4 tsp freshly ground black pepper.

---

1 slice sautéed bacon, chopped

1 scallion, chopped

1/2 tsp roasted garlic puree*

1/4 cup red wine

1/4 tsp black pepper

---

1 scallion, chopped

1/4 cup Madeira wine

1 Tb apple butter

1/2 tsp roasted garlic*

1/4 tsp black pepper

---

1 Tb mushroom Duxelles*

1/4 cup dry white wine (substitute red wine)

1/4 cup beef or venison stock or brown stock*

---

1 scallion, chopped

1/4 cup roasted tomato*, chopped

1/2 tsp roasted garlic*

1/4 cup red wine

1/4 tsp black pepper

1 scallion, chopped
1 Tb Italian parsley, chopped

1/4 cup dry white wine
2 Tb ketchup
1/2 tsp roasted garlic*
1/4 tsp black pepper

---

1 slice sautéed bacon, chopped
1 scallion, chopped
1 Tb Hot Sweet Chili Garlic Sauce*
2 Tb venison or beef stock*

Sauteed Venison Liver

Soak 1/2 + lb liver in water; cut in 1/2" to 3/4" pieces.

Saute in 2 Tb coconut oil until rare. Salt. Then add the sauce and boil down quickly, stirring. A wok works well for this. Serve medium rare to medium. There should be some pink.

Sauce:

2 Tb dijon-style mustard
1 tsp of brown sugar or coconut sugar
1 tsp gluten-free worchestershire sauce
2 tsp Balsamic vinegar
1 tsp lemon juice
1/2 tsp black pepper

Serve with onions browned in coconut oil. Serves two.

Sauteed Venison Liver with Green Peppers

1 lb venison liver, 1/2" dice (or substitute beef or pork liver)
1 cup julienned carrots, 1- 1½" long
2 green bell or other sweet peppers, 1/2" dice
1/4 cup coconut oil
1 Tb ginger, minced
3 scallions, chopped
1 Tb gluten-free Szechuan hot bean paste or hot chili paste
4 cloves garlic, minced
3-4" dried orange peel, soaked and minced
1 Tb fermented black beans, soaked and mashed (or black bean paste)
1 Tb gluten-free soy sauce, tamari sauce or coconut aminos
1 Tb dry sherry
2 tsp toasted oriental sesame oil

Saute green peppers and carrots in 2 Tb coconut oil in a wok until they are well done and beginning to brown. Remove. Add 2 more Tb coconut oil and saute the ginger briefly, then add the Szechuan hot bean paste, black beans, garlic and orange peel and cook for a minute or two, then add the liver and saute on high heat until just rare. Add soy sauce and sherry and return the carrots and peppers to the wok and heat through. Off heat, and add the sesame oil. Serves four. You could substitute beef or pork liver.

SautJed Lamb Patties with Rosemay, Onions and Peppers

1 lb organic lamb burger
1/2 cup onion, minced
1 tsp roasted garlic puree

1/2 cup bell or other sweet pepper, minced
1/2 tsp freshly ground black pepper
1/2 tsp salt
1 egg
3-4 drops rosemary oil
2 Tb coconut oil or organic lard

Saute the onion and bell pepper in 1 Tb coconut oil until the onion is translucent and beginning to brown. Set the pan aside. Cool and combine well with the lamb burger, garlic, black pepper, salt, egg, and rosemary oil. It is best to kneed with your hand to mix thoroughly. Form into patties and add another 1 Tb coconut oil to the pan. Saute on high heat, browning the surfaces. Medium rare is good. Serves four. Top with this sauce, warmed:

1/4 cup organic, gluten-free tomato ketchup and 2 Tb Hot Sweet Chili Garlic Sauce*

Braised Venison Hearts

Two deer hearts, or one elk heart cut in 3/4" – 1" pieces. I've seen people leave the heart and liver behind in the field. Waste not, want not. (The tongue can also be saved, and the kidneys.) This would be a good hearty dish to serve following a winter ski outing, prepared in advance and warmed up.

Dredge in

   1/2 cup gluten-free flour
   1/2 tsp salt
   1/2 tsp black pepper

Brown in

   1/4 cup Tb avocado oil
   1 Tb coconut oil

Remove from the pan, add more oil and saute until brown

    2 small onions or one large, in 1/2" pieces

Add

    1/2 cup leeks, sliced
    1/2 cup roasted tomatoes, chopped or 1 cup puree or chopped
        fresh or canned tomatoes
    1/2 cup celery, chopped
    1/2 cup dried wild mushrooms such as oyster, fairy ring, cepe.
        Soak and save the water. Or use 2 cups sliced fresh wild
        mushrooms, browned with the onions. (You could substitute
        supermarket crimini mushrooms.)
    4 garlic cloves, crushed
    1 cup green French lentils, soaked overnight and drained.
    3 cups venison or beef stock*
    1 cup red wine
    1 tsp salt

Tie in cheesecloth and add

    1/2 cup Italian cooking parsley
    1 sprig fresh thyme
    1 bay leaf
    1/2 tsp black peppercorns
    2 tsp fresh sage

Return the venison hearts to the pan, bring to a simmer and cook 1 hour, partially covered. Stir frequently to avoid sticking. Add a little more water if necessary.

After 1 hour, add 2 cups sliced carrots, and cook another hour. Serves 6-8.

Barbequed Venison Ribs

Venison ribs can also be barbequed, as with the pork BBQ. To do this, I use a Sawzall type reciprocating saw to cut the ribs into manageable pieces, 4-5" long while still attached to the carcass. Separate into serving size pieces. Then I apply the rub and marinate overnight, or for a couple of days. Then I pre-cook them in a 250 degree oven, covered, with this sauce:

> 1 onion, finely chopped, sauteed in 2 Tb coconut oil
> 1/2 cup roasted tomato*, pureed
> 1/2 cup dry white wine
> 1/2 cup red wine
> 1 tsp dried oregano
> 1/2 tsp thyme
> 1 tsp salt
> 1 tsp black pepper
> 1 cup beef or venison stock*
> 2 cups water
> 1 Tb honey

Then I smoke them in the pit barbeque for another 3 hours at approximately 250 degrees, applying the mop (page 140) regularly and slathering with barbeque sauce for the last half hour or so.

Since it is neither possible nor desireable to remove all the fat, be aware that venison fat is like lamb fat in that it is not agreeable to the palate once it is cooled. I recommend placing a chafing dish on the table to keep it warm, and guests should take one piece at a time. Venison fat is said to become rancid in the freezer, so the ribs should be cooked while still fresh if possible.

Basic Venison Marinade

2 cups red wine
1 onion, minced
2 cloves garlic, smashed
1/2 tsp pepper
1/2 tsp marjoram (or thyme or rosemary)
1/2 tsp Worcestershire sauce (gluten free is available)
1/4 cup olive oil

If the meat is tough or gamey, add 1/4 cup balsamic or red wine vinegar. Marinate at least 4 hours or overnight.

Backwoods Critter Ragout

You can use: Porcupine, raccoon, squirrel, woodchuck or rock chuck, rabbit, bear etc. Cut up whatever critters you have into serving size pieces. Coat with gluten-free flour and salt and pepper. Use 2 pounds or so.

Prepare and set aside
2 cups sliced carrots
2 cups sliced celery
Saute 1 chopped onion
2 chopped garlic cloves

in 2 Tb avocado oil and/or rendered bacon fat until onions are translucent. Remove and set aside.

Saute critter pieces in remaining oil or rendered bacon fat until brown. Use more oil if needed. Remove.

1/2 cup dried cepe mushrooms, soaked in 1 cup water

Saute 2 + cups sliced fresh mushrooms, preferably wild, until brown. Chanterelles, fairy ring mushrooms, oyster mushrooms, sweet tooths, meadow mushrooms, or morels would be good choices. If using 1 cup dried wild mushrooms instead, reconstitute in warm water then squeeze. Save the water, and briefly saute the reconstituted mushrooms. You could also use Duxelles.

Combine the critters, mushrooms, onion, garlic with:

1 cup diced turnip
1 small parsnip, sliced
1 herb bouquet (Italian parsley, thyme, bay leaf, black peppercorns, oregano)
1 ham hock
2 cups red wine (You could use dry white wine with young raccoon or rabbit. The jackrabbit is the only north American hare, and it has dark meat, so you would use red wine.)
3 cups beef stock or game stock* (chicken stock with young raccoon or rabbit)
3 diced tomatoes (or 1 11 oz can tomatoes or 1 cup roasted tomatoes, chopped)
1 tsp salt

Simmer for 2-3 hours, until the meat is nearly tender. Add the carrots and celery and cook an additional hour until everything is tender. Serve.

I've seen jackrabbits which had tularemia, and these had to be discarded. If the liver has large obvious yellow lesions, walk away from it. This is why it is a good idea to wear rubber gloves when field dressing animals.

Sauces
etc.

Introduction to Sauces

Sauces are useful for quick and easy dishes and for dishes where the meat, fish or vegetable is cooked quickly and not over cooked. The sauce is added at the conclusion, or served separately with the entree. Sauces can also be poured over food prior to baking, as with crepes. (In addition, many of the dishes in this book effectively create a sauce in which the meat and vegetables are cooked.)

Many sauces are included with the entrees listed under separate chapters. Here are more free-standing sauces.

Many sauces can be served with a variety of different meats, fish or vegetables, according to convenience. A sauce might equally be served with pork or fish or chicken, or with lamb or beef or venison, depending on your tastes and available ingredients. It may be that a simple modification, such as substituting one stock for another, can serve to adapt a sauce to different meats. Be creative.

An absolutely fabulous quick and easy mayonnaise can be made with the food processor, using melted coconut oil mixed with avocado oil. I have presented a recipe on page . Coconut oil does have some anti-microbial properties, so coconut mayonnaise lasts longer than regular mayonnaise, and may perhaps help avoid problems with Salmonella poisoning from raw eggs. Alternately, to avoid the use of raw eggs and produce a longer-lasting mayonnaise, use powdered organic eggs according to the recipe in Helen Witty's *The Good Food Cookbook*.

Similarly, Hollandaise and Bearnaise type sauces can be made using coconut oil instead of butter. If anything, these coconut sauces are more stable than butter-based sauces. I have developed a coconut-based, huckleberry flavored Hollandaise), and two sauces based on Bearnaise.

Gluten and Dairy-Free Roux

Roux is classically made with butter and regular wheat flour. It is used to thicken sauces or soups, etc., in French cooking. I found that a good, functional roux can be made with gluten-free flour mix and virgin unrefined coconut oil mixed 50:50 with avocado oil.

To make it, cook 1 Tb coconut oil and 1 Tb avocado oil with 2 Tb gluten free flour mix. (I used Namaste gluten free organic „Perfect Flour Blend" from Costco.) For brown roux, cook on low heat for 8-10 minutes until it is nicely brown, stirring nearly constantly. Whisk it into the sauce or ragout or soup you're making and simmer for 5 minutes to thicken. This is enough to thicken about a half gallon of ragout.

Blond roux would be made similarly, but cooked only long enough to begin to get a yellowish color. This is used in dishes involving coconut cream sauces for poultry or fish or fricasses, or for soups.

You could make a large batch of roux and freeze individual packets, 1 Tb each, wrapped in wax paper then in aluminum foil. Place them in a baggie and label and date it.

Basic Brown Sauce

Saute 2 Tb chopped scallions or shallots in 2 Tb coconut oil briefly, then add 1/2 cup dry white wine and 2 Tb Madeira wine and reduce briefly.

Then add 1 ½ cup organic beef broth plus 1 Tb commercial beef stock base, or use homemade concentrated brown beef or venison stock or even demiglace sauce.

Add

> 1 small carrot, sliced
> 1/2 cup diced celery
> 1/2 tsp tomato paste or 1 tsp tomato puree
> 1 crushed garlic clove
> 1/2 tsp fresh thyme or 1/4 tsp dried
> 1/2 tsp fresh marjoram or 1/4 tsp dried
> 1 Tb fresh Italian parsley, chopped
> 1/2 small bay leaf
> 1 allspice berry
> 1/4 tsp black pepper
> Add a pinch of crumbled saffron, soaked in 1 Tb warm water (optional)

Simmer 30 min. Remove herb bag then strain.

Simmer 5 minutes more prior to serving. Thicken with arrowroot or cornstarch if needed. Salt to taste.

See also Wild Mushroom Brown Sauce.

Hot Sweet Chili Garlic Sauce

This Thai- inspired sauce is nice to have on hand as an easy start to any number of other (secondary) sauces, or you can use it as is to top chicken or fish. Several of the recipes in this book incorporte it.

> 1 quart rice vinegar or white wine vinegar
> 2 quarts xylitol or coconut sugar
> 1 cup minced fresh garlic (divided in two)
> 2 tsp salt

Combine with half the garlic, stir, and bring to a boil in a saucepan, then simmer on medium low for at least an hour, until thick and syrupy. Near the end of cooking, add the remaining 1/2 cup garlic, and cook another half hour. Remove from the heat and add

1/2 cup hot chili paste or more to taste (can be purchased).

Let cool, then bottle and refrigerate. It keeps well.

Sauce for Barbequed Pork (or fish or chicken)

2 Tb chopped shallots, sauteed in coconut oil

Add:

1/2 cup grape jelly or elderberry jelly
1/4 cup Madeira wine
2 Tb Balsamic vinegar
1/2 tsp salt
1 tsp roasted garlic puree
1/3 cup water

Simmer 5 minutes to thicken.

Optional additions:

2 roasted (blackened) and peeled red bell peppers or other sweet
    pepper, pureed.
1/3 cup thick coconut milk (for fish or chicken breasts).

Coconut Huckleberry Hollandaise Sauce

This sauce is prepared in a food processor with the metal blade. This is somewhat easier than the traditional method. It substitutes coconut oil for butter and is fairly stable.

Combine in a small sauce pan:

> 1 Tb lemon (or lime) juice
> 2 Tb water
> 1/4 tsp freshly ground white pepper
> 1/4 tsp salt

Reduce over medium heat to about 2 Tb and set aside.

Combine in a food processor:

> The reduced lemon juice
> 3 egg yolks
> 1 Tb huckleberry jam (or syrup)

and process for several seconds. Scrape the sides and process again.

Heat 3/4 cup virgin unprocessed coconut oil to 240-250 degrees. Start the processor. Using a metal funnel, slowly drizzle the hot coconut oil through the center opening.

It will gradually form the emulsion and thicken. If it is too thick, very slowly drizzle in very small amounts of warm water until it is as you like it.

Keep warm in a heat proof glass bowl over hot water (off heat). Serve with fish filets, pork loin steaks, or chicken, pheasant or grouse breasts. Makes about 1 cup. Serves 4 to 6.

Coconut Rosemary Bearnaise

A Bearnaise style sauce made in the food processor, with coconut oil instead of butter.

Combine in a small sauce pan and simmer 10 minutes

  1/4 cup white wine vinegar
  1/4 cup dry white vermouth or dry white wine
  1/4 cup fresh or frozen rosemary leaves, mashed in a mortar

Strain and discard the rosemary leaves.

Add

  1 Tb minced shallots or scallions
  1/4 tsp salt
  big pinch black pepper
  1/2 tsp roasted garlic puree
  3 drops rosemary oil

Cook down slowly until you have about 2 Tb. Set aside.

Heat 3/4 cup virgin coconut oil in a small sauce pan until it reaches 240-250 degrees on a candy thermometer.

Place in the bowl of the food processor

  3 egg yolks

Using the metal blade, blend the yolks briefly, then while it is still running, slowly drizzle in the vinegar reduction, above. Use a metal funnel placed in the center hole of the lid.

Then, while it is still running, slowly drizzle in the hot oil. It will gradually become thick. If it is too thick, very slowly drizzle in a small amount of warm water until it is as thick as you want it.

Keep warm in a heat-proof glass bowl set in a basin of fairly hot water (off the heat). Try to serve it soon, if not immediately. Makes about 1 cup.

Don's Sauce Montagne

A Bearnaise style sauce made in the food processor, with coconut oil instead of butter.

Combine

> 1 Tb Balsamic vinegar
> 3 Tb white wine vinegar
> 1/4 cup dry white vermouth
> 1 Tb minced shallots or scallions
> 1/4 tsp salt
> 1/4 tsp black pepper
> 1/2 tsp roasted, ground Szechuan peppercorns*
> 1 tsp ancho chili powder
> 1/4 tsp cayenne pepper
> 1/2 tsp roasted garlic puree*

Cook down slowly until you have about 2 Tb. Set aside.

Heat 3/4 cup virgin coconut oil in a small sauce pan until it reaches 240-250 degrees on a candy thermometer.

Place in the bowl of the food processor:

> 3 egg yolks

Using the metal blade, blend the yolks briefly, then while it is still running, slowly drizzle in the vinegar reduction, above. Use a metal funnel placed in the center hole of the lid.

Then, while it is still running, drizzle in the hot oil. It will gradually become thick. If it is too thick, very slowly drizzle in a small amount of warm water until it is as thick as you want it. Keep warm in a heat-proof glass bowl set in a basin of fairly hot water (off the heat). Try to serve it soon, if not immediately. Makes about 1 cup. Serves 4-6.

Good with grilled venison steaks, or lamb, bison, or beef.

Coconut- Cashew Cream Sauce (Non-Dairy)

1 large shallot, chopped or 1-2 scallions

1 Tb coconut oil

1/2 cup raw cashew butter (or puree your own)

1 cup canned thick coconut milk

1 ½ cups chicken bone broth or good chicken stock (if this is to be used for fish, use fish stock)

1/4 cup dry white wine

2 Tb cognac or brandy

1/2 tsp salt

1/2 tsp freshly ground white pepper

Saute the shallot or scallions in coconut oil.

Add the cashew butter, coconut milk, white wine, stock, salt, and pepper. Mix thoroughly until smooth and bring to a simmer, partially covered. Cook for 15-20 minutes, until thick and flavorful. Taste for seasoning.

(optional- 1/2 tsp sweet paprika)
(optional- sauté 1 cup fresh sliced mushrooms with the shallot)

Serve with sautéed chicken breast, grouse or pheasant breast, or fish filets. This can also be used to make crepes.

Coconut Mayonnaise

> 1 whole egg
> 2 egg yolks
> 1/2 tsp Dijon style mustard
> 1/2 tsp salt

Combine and blend in your food processor with the metal blade for one minute. Add

> 1 tsp white wine vinegar

Combine in a 2 cup measuring cup

> 2/3 cup coconut oil, just melted (not too hot)
> 1 1/3 cup avocado oil

With the machine running, drizzle the oils in a thin stream through the center hole. A funnel will help with this. It will begin to thicken. Turn off the machine, scrape down the sides, add

> 1 tsp white wine vinegar

Start the machine again and continue drizzling the oils in.

Bottle in a sterile jar or two and keep refrigerated. The coconut oil is anti- microbial and will help to keep this fresh longer than mayonnaise would normally last. It should also help ease concerns about Salmonella poisoning from using raw eggs.

Optional:

Additional flavorings can be added, as you wish. You could incorporate mixtures of chopped herbs such as tarragon, chervil, parsley, chives, basil, roasted garlic puree), roasted tomato puree, or curry powder.

Chervil Coconut Sauce

Serve with chicken breast or pork chops. Sauté two chicken breasts or pork chops until lightly browned, then combine with the sauce and bake for 20 minutes at 350 degrees.

Combine

> 1 tsp roasted garlic*
> 1/4 cup minced fresh chervil herb
> 2 scallions, chopped
> 1 Tb raw cashew butter
> 1/3 cup dry white wine
> 1 cup thick coconut milk
> 1/4 tsp salt
> 1/4 tsp freshly ground white pepper

Combine with the chicken or pork, then bake for 20 minutes at 350 degrees.

Serves two.

Shrimp Sauce

> 1/2 cup avocado oil
> Shells from 3 lb shrimp.

Saute until brown and crisp, taking care not to burn.

Add

> 1 cup applejack or calvados; flambe.

Add water to cover, along with

> 1 bay leaf
> A sprig of thyme
> 1/2 onion, sliced.

Cook for 1 ½ hours, then strain. Add

> 1/2 cup chopped shallots
> 1 ½ cups white wine
> 2 cups of fish stock
> 5 cloves chopped garlic, or use 1 Tb roasted garlic paste
> 1/4 cup fresh tarragon, chopped
> 1/2 tsp ground star anise

Reduce to about 1 ½ cup.

Add 1 can coconut milk (thick) in increments, boiling down each time – it should end up thick and concentrated.

Add

> 1/2 tsp saffron, soaked
> 1/2 tsp freshly ground white pepper

Optional: 1 cup chopped sauteed fresh morel mushrooms, or chanterelles, sweet tooths, or shrimp russulas or 1/2 cup duxelles*.

Can be used as is as a topping for fish, or you could add 1/2 lb cooked shrimp, coarsely chopped (along with the mushrooms), and use it to fill morel or other mushrooms prior to baking, or as a filling for crepes, or as a topping for cooked fish.

Quick Sauce for Steamed Veggies or Sauteed Fish

1 Tb gluten free sweet Indonesian soy sauce
1 tsp roasted, ground Szechuan pepper
1/4 cup orange (or lime, etc) marmalade
1/4 cup fresh orange juice

Bring to a simmer, cook 2-3 min.

Pour over steamed cauliflower, broccoli, or carrots, or over sauteed, broiled or baked fish filets.

For two servings.

Spicy Coconut Tarragon-Pecan Sauce

Combine

1/4 cup fresh tarragon, finely minced (or substitute basil)
2 Tb chopped pecans
1/4 cup coconut oil
2 Tb hot sweet chili garlic sauce*
1/2 tsp freshly ground black pepper
2 tsp freshly ground pan roasted Szechuan peppercorns*
1/2 tsp salt

Heat to a simmer and pour over grilled steaks, pork chops or fish filets.

Serves 3-4.

Thai Style Hot Sweet Coconut Lime Sauce

For stir-fried veggies. Also good with fish.

Combine

> 1 cup coconut milk
> 1/4 cup Hot Sweet Thai Chili Garlic Sauce*
> 2 Tb lime juice
> 1 Tb black soy sauce, tamari, or coconut aminos
> 2 tsp lime zest (you might include a fresh frozen kaffir lime leaf or two, finely minced)
> 2 drops lemongrass oil

Stir-fry veggies** in coconut oil, then add the sauce and

Bring to a simmer and cook for 3-4 minutes. Then add

> 2 tsp arrowroot powder (or non-GMO cornstarch) dissolved inw 1 Tb water to thicken.

**Good choices would be pak choi, broccoli, cauliflower, fresh beans, fresh peppers, carrots, snow peas or sugar snap peas.

Turkey Sauce

Roast (or smoke) one turkey or turkey breast. If applicable, deglaze the roasting pan with

> 1/2 cup dry white wine; cook down, scraping, then add
> 4 cups chicken (or turkey) stock*

In a heavy saucepan, saute

　1 small chopped onion
　2 cloves chopped garlic in
　1 Tb coconut oil until translucent and slightly browned.

Transfer the contents of the roasting pan to the saucepan (or just add the wine and stock) and add

　1 Tb apricot jam or 1/2 cup dried, chopped candy cap mushrooms
　1 Tb fresh tarragon, chopped
　1 tsp rubbed sage or minced fresh sage
　1/2 cup coconut milk (or almond or hemp milk)
　1/2 tsp freshly ground white pepper

Simmer 20 minutes, strain if desired, then thicken with arrowroot.

Roasted Red Pepper Coconut Sauce

Serve with grilled salmon filets or steaks (or trout or other fish). Serves four.

Charbroil 2 red bell peppers (or Sweet Italia) until the skin is black, then peel and chop. It sometimes works best to peel under cold running water.

　2 shallots, chopped
　4 cloves chopped garlic (or use 2 tsp roasted garlic puree)
　1 Tb coconut oil

Saute the chopped shallots and garlic in the coconut oil until beginning to brown.

Then puree the peppers, shallots and garlic with

> 1 Tb chopped fresh basil (or substitute fresh tarragon)
> 1/2 cup dry white wine
> 1/2 tsp salt
> 2 Tb maple syrup
> 1/2 cup thick coconut milk

Place in a pan and simmer 10 min., stirring frequently.

Almond – Orange Sauce

Served over sautéed fish filets, sautéed chicken breast, or pork chops.

> 1/4 cup orange juice
> 2-3 drops orange oil or 1 tsp orange zest
> 1 tsp almond butter
> 2 Tb toasted, slivered almonds
> 2 Tb dry white wine
> 1/4 tsp white pepper
> 1/4 tsp salt
> 2 scallions or shallots, chopped
> 1 Tb coconut oil

Sauté the meat, remove from the pan, then sauté the shallots or scallions, and add the sauce and deglaze the pan, scraping. Serve over the meat. This is an amount sufficient for one or two servings.

Huckleberry – Pistachio – Chili Sauce

Serve over sautéed fish filets, chicken breast, or pork chops. Combine and warm. Sufficient for two servings. Multiply as needed.

1 Tb coconut oil
1 Tb huckleberry jam
1 Tb Hot Sweet Chili Garlic Sauce*
1 Tb pistachios, chopped
1 tsp Dijon-style mustard
1/4 tsp salt
1/4 tsp freshly ground black pepper

Desserts

Chocolate Coconut Pecan Minglement

Per serving

  2 Tb coconut oil
  1 Tb good dark chocolate, broken or 2 tsp raw cacao powder
  2 tsp agave nectar
  2 Tb chopped pecans (or walnuts)
  1 Tb pecan butter
  1/2 dropper stevia

Optional

  – A few drops of orange oil
  – 1 Tb raisins

Melt and mix together, then refrigerate to set up.

Optional — Top with Coconut Sauce*.

As time has passed I find myself less and less interested in making fancy, involved desserts. These Minglements which I have developed are very quick and easy to make, especially if you skip the sauce. And, the combination of chocolate and coconut oil, in particular, is very healthy. Staves off Alzheimer's, for one thing.

Almond Walnut Coconut Peppermint Minglement

Combine, per serving

  2 Tb coconut oil
  2 tsp almond butter
  2 tsp agave nectar or honey

1/2 dropper stevia

1 tsp heavy coconut milk or coconut cream or coconut manna

2 Tb raisins

1/4 cup chopped walnuts

3 drops peppermint oil

Mix and refrigerate to set up

Optional – Serve with coconut sauce made with Amaretto liqueur.

Chocolate- Hazelnut Coconut Minglement

Combine

1/4 cup chopped toasted peeled hazelnuts

2 tsp Frangelico liqueur

1/4 cup coconut oil

1 dropper stevia

2 tsp blue agave nectar

1 Tb raw cacao powder or dark chocolate

Refrigerate to set up. Serve with optional Frangelico- flavored Coconut Minglement Sauce*. Serves two.

Coconut – Almond Minglement

Per serving

2 Tb coconut oil or coconut manna

2 tsp honey

2 tsp almond butter

1 dropper stevia

2 Tb slivered almonds, carefully toasted in a dry frying pan
1 Tb coconut cream or thick coconut milk

Optional- 1 tsp cacao powder. Melt ingredients together, mixing, then refrigerate until set up. Serve with coconut sauce* made with Amaretto liqeuer.

Coconut Sauces for Minglements

Combine

> 1 cup thick canned coconut milk
> 2 Tb coconut sugar or xylitol

Bring to a boil and cook on medium, stirring, until it is thick and reduced by half.

Add

> 2 Tb dark rum or other gluten-free liqueur
> 1/2 tsp vanilla extract

Simmer an additional 3-4 minutes.

Refrigerate until ready to serve.

Rather than rum, you could use Grand Marnier (orange cognac), or Frangelico (hazelnut liqueur), Amaretto di Sarona (almond liqueur), Calvados (apple liqueur) or unblended straight applejack, or other gluten-free liqueurs. Serve over a matching minglement of your choice.

About 6-8 servings.

Gooseberry Conserve with Mixed Fruits

3 cups green gooseberries
1 3/4 cups xylitol or coconut sugar
1/2 cup chopped dried dates or dried apricots
1/2 cup golden raisins
1 cup strawberries
2 Tb orange marmalade

Combine all ingredients except the strawberries in a sauce pan and cook on medium heat, stirring frequently until the sugar is dissolved, then lower the heat and cook 15 minutes; then stir in the strawberries and cook another 10+ minutes until it is reduced and thickened. Stir frequently.

Can the conserve in 1 cup jars in a boiling water bath or store in the refrigerator.

Pears in Nanking Cherry Sauce

2 unripe pears, quartered

Combine and simmer

1 cup white wine
1/2+ cup Nanking cherries
2 Tb brandy or cognac
2 Tb lemon juice
1+ Tb coconut sugar or xylitol, depending on how sweet the wine is.
4 pieces orange peel and
3 whole allspice cloves, tied in cheesecloth.

Simmer until the pears are tender to the fork, remove the pears and cherries and reserve. Remove and discard the orange peel and allspice cloves.

Add

1/4 cup coconut cream or thick coconut milk, or coconut manna.

Reduce by a third and add pears and cherries and toss to coat. Serve cool.

Serves four. Substitute dried cherries or fresh or frozen pie cherries for the Nanking cherries.

Grandma Miller's Mincemeat

A food processor (such as the Cuisinart) is essential for this...

5 lb finely chopped lean venison (or use beef)
2 lb beef suet (not fat), ground
5 quarts minced apples
3 large oranges, zested, then peeled and chopped
1 Tb grated orange zest
3 lemons, zested, then peeled and chopped
1 Tb grated lemon zest
2 lb seeded raisins
2 lb dried currants
2 lb coconut sugar
4 cups xylitol plus 1/3 cup organic molasses
2 Tb ground cinnamon
2 tsp ground allspice
1 Tb ground mace
2 tsp ground cloves
2 tsp ground coriander seed
2 Tb salt

2 quarts boiling organic apple cider
1 quart beef broth
1 cup white wine vinegar

Using a large deep acid resistant roasting pan, bake covered for 2 ½ hours at 350 degrees.

While still hot, can in quart jars in a boiling water bath for 30 minutes or freeze in quart jars.

This is used to make mincemeat pies.

Apple-Coconut Yoghurt Cup

Per serving. Combine

1/2 cup chopped organic apple
1 Tb apple butter
2 Tb unsweetened cultured coconut milk
1/4 tsp cinnamon
1/2 dropper stevia
1 Tb chopped walnuts

Strawberries with Chocolate Sauce

For two servings,

Combine

1/4 cup coconut oil
1 Tb dark chocolate, grated, or 1 Tb cacao powder
1/4 cup thick coconut milk
2 tsp agave nectar

1 dropper stevia
1 Tb brandy or cognac

Heat together until melted. Allow to cool, pour over

1-1 ½ cups strawberries, sliced. Serve.

This sauce could also be served over Minglements.

Sweet Coconut – Cashew Cream Sauce

Combine

1/3 cup raw cashew butter
1 can thick canned coconut milk
1/2 cup port wine
1/4 cup brandy or cognac
1/3+ cup xylitol or coconut sugar
1 dropper stevia
1/2 cup white wine
1/2 cup thin coconut milk
1 tsp vanilla extract

(Optional- 2 Tb dark chocolate, grated, or 2 Tb powder)
(Optional- 1/4 cup huckleberry jam or other fruit jam)

Simmer for 10 minutes, stirring frequently. Cool. Puree with a hand immersion blender. Thin with a bit of thin coconut milk, carefully, if desired.

Serve over fresh strawberries, blueberries, peaches, etc. Could also be used to top a fruit tart, if made thick.

Index